mascord efficient living

Your Guide to Building a Sustainable Lifestyle
with Alan Mascord Design Associates, Inc.

AMDA PRESS

Portland, Oregon

AMDA PRESS

President: *Alan Mascord*

Vice President: *Donna Mascord*

General Manager: *Jon Epley*

Publisher: *Amy Fullwiler*

Editorial Directors: *Gary Higginbotham*
Matthew Daby

Creative Director: *Diane Arthur Kukish*

Graphic Design: *Gary Higginbotham*
Kim Campeau

Website/Multimedia Design: *Kevin Banton, Jeff Eblen*

Customer Service Manager: *Joelle Irvine*

Director of Home Design: *Eric Schnell*

Plan Production Manager: *Marie Adams*

Senior Drafting Technician: *Randy Voeller*

Writers: *Gary Higginbotham, Matthew Daby*
David Cohen, Mary Afeman

Sketchup Models: *Alan Mascord, Dave Reid,*
Kevin Banton, Kim Campeau,
Joseph Sharkey

Illustrator: *Aaron Johnson, Gary Higginbotham*

Photographers: *Bob Greenspan, Alan Mascord*
Gary Higginbotham, Marcus Berg
Christine Banton, Cheryl Muhr
Aerolist Photographers, Inc., Steve Mason

Customer Service: *(503) 225-9161*
sales@mascordefficientliving.com

To Order Plans: (800) 411-0231

Website Address: www.mascordefficientliving.com

foreword
by Sarah Susanka

When I released *The Not So Big House* in 1998, the first in a series of books that is changing the way people think about "home", I knew I was telling readers that they needed a type of house that was pretty hard to find—especially in the existing home plan market. At the time, you could page through hundreds of home plan books and magazines and find not a single design that met the standards I emphasized—a house that favors quality over quantity, a house that eliminates the rarely used formal rooms, a house with both character and integrity, and a house that's sustainably made.

It's not too surprising, then, that one of the most common inquiries I receive from readers is *"Where can I find more plans that reflect the layout characteristics you describe in your books, with every space designed to be lived in every day."* Up until now there have been few options for me to point them toward, but the situation is changing. I'm delighted to be able to

introduce you to this wonderful collection of green home plans, designed by one of this country's leading home designers. Alan Mascord had a vision thirty years ago to create well designed and energy efficient homes for all Americans. Today we've come to recognize that these characteristics are fundamental to green building and to sustainable design. He was designing *green* homes before we'd even coined the term.

What is remarkable about the plans that Alan Mascord has developed over the past three decades, and which he is now making available to you through this book and DVD, is that in addition to being both beautiful and sensibly designed for the way we *really* live, they are also designed to the highest standards of green building, meeting the requirements for LEED® (Leadership in Energy and Environmental Design) certification and the National Green Building Standard™. You'll notice that each of the houses herein even has an Efficient Living Rating to help you select a house that is both sustainable *and* enjoyable to live in.

You make a house into home by personalizing it, and all the tools provided for you here will allow you to do just that. Together with Whirlpool Corporation, a company that has for many years been at the cutting edge of green design, and with Google SketchUp, a computer modeling program that allows you to visualize and interact with the house plans you are interested in, this book and DVD provide a veritable treasure trove of green home designs for truly sustainable living.

For many years I've encouraged people to pick the house they choose to build not just from a floor plan, which tells only a small part of the story, but with information about the heights of things as well—the third dimension. As you'll see, the tools that SketchUp

offers allow you to see more completely what you will be building before you begin, and make the entire selection process both easier and a lot more fun. For those who want to make the interior of the house even more personal, over the coming months, I will be collaborating with Mascord to introduce some "not so big" interior detail packages for a few of the houses in this book. You can take a look at these interior detail options by visiting either **www.mascordefficientliving.com** or **www.notsobighouse.com**.

So I hope you'll enjoy the adventure in house design that you are about to embark upon. There's so much we can do to make our houses more comfortable, and more like "home", but to do so we need tools like the ones you'll find here to help you see in all three dimensions what your house will look and feel like once it's built. After a few minutes of exploration, I think you'll agree that there's nothing else like this book and DVD on the market. Have fun, and keep in mind that living well means living sustainably, and it all begins at home.

—Sarah Susanka, FAIA

Architect and author of *The Not So Big House* series, *Home By Design*, and *The Not So Big Life*

Alan Mascord Design Associates—Designing Homes Sensibly

Going Green, Living Smart

Thank you for your interest in this extraordinary collection of thoughts, ideas and homes.

I've reached a point in my life as a home designer, father, and grandfather, where I've become all the more mindful of the future. Compounded by news of global events and consciously thoughtful of our collective impact on the environment, the recent birth of my first grandchild, Chloe, instilled me with a deep awareness that the world belongs to our beloved children, their children, and generations yet to come. The impact we have already had on our environment certainly affects us in serious and visible ways— long term repercussions of past environmental abuse are present and scientifically documented in the rock on the ground, the air we breathe and the water we drink. I am not alone in being aware. The construction industry is also aware and responding by producing certification programs to enable responsible homeowners and builders to quantify their efforts to build more sustainably.

We at AMDA have been responsibly designing high quality homes for over thirty years, and, in that time, the efficiency, durability, and livability of the homes we design has been of utmost importance. Consistent with our philosophy of *Ease and Excellence*, we're adding tools to enable our clients to make smart, responsible choices.

Our Efficient Living program offers a simple and effective way to make smart choices and communicate them directly to everyone involved in the construction of the home; in a manner that construction professionals are used to seeing. This package compliments national certification programs and will instruct you on how to build your efficient home to exceed certification standards, save energy, give advice on material usage, and suggest key ways to reduce your consumption. In addition, we've compiled a collection of some of the most elegant and striking designs we've ever created across a wide range of styles and applied our principles to them, proving that you don't have to sacrifice luxury or personal taste to lessen your impact on the environment.

No company shares our combination of efficiency and style more than Whirlpool Corporation. We are proud to partner with Whirlpool, the industry leader in ENERGY STAR compliance, in the design of this collection. The following home plans, coupled with our efficient living program, will contribute to our environment's future health through the widespread incorporation of sustainable building practices, materials and appliances. I sincerely thank you for considering an efficient home, for building responsibly, and for protecting the future for our children.

Best Regards,

Alan Mascord, *President*
Alan Mascord Design Associates, Inc.

Table of Contents

How to Use this Book

Mascord Efficient Living is about much more than sustainability. It's about sustainability with style. Living efficiently need not be a detriment to your chosen lifestyle, it can be a huge advantage. *Mascord Efficient Living* home plans add to that advantage by making it easy to build an efficient home to national green building standards. Information, details and specifications provided in our plan package are consistent with certification guidelines, and delivered to the jobsite in a manner consistent with traditional construction practices.

Our aim with this book, accompanying DVD and online library is to provide basic information, tips and suggestions covering all elements of building a stylish, efficient home—and living in one thereafter. Building an efficient home or living an efficient lifestyle is about making smart choices; the information in this book is intended as a guide to making those choices.

This book is designed to be flexible to use. Read it all the way through or jump to the parts that interest you most. Flip through pages and pick up tips along the way. In each chapter, you will find text describing the elements to consider within the confines of the subject at hand. Following each chapter are home plans to consider for your own efficient home—introduced by a real world example of how all the concepts of Mascord Efficient Living have been put into practice.

The Efficient Living Rating

Although you may build an efficient living home without getting it certified, each home built to national certification standards scores points to acheive a certain level of compliance within the chosen track. Awards vary in degree from 'Certified' to 'Platinum' or 'Emerald,'. depending on which certification program you choose. Following our standard specifications, and with a few location or installation specific variables, your *Mascord Efficient Living* home will score a pre-calculated number of points. To help you determine an expected level of certification, without being program specific, we have devised an Efficient Living Rating. On a scale of one to five, with five being the highest, the number of leaves 🍃 pertains to the relative level you might expect to achieve if you build this home (in a preferrable location) using our standard details. Options, designed into the system, can be implemented to improve your efficiency and increase your award level.

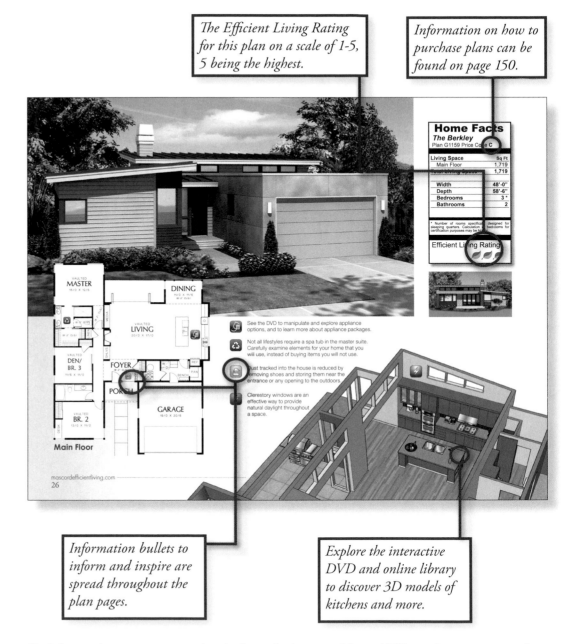

The Efficient Living Rating for this plan on a scale of 1-5, 5 being the highest.

Information on how to purchase plans can be found on page 150.

Information bullets to inform and inspire are spread throughout the plan pages.

Explore the interactive DVD and online library to discover 3D models of kitchens and more.

Each home plan page contains details about the home, a *Mascord Efficient Living* rating, and additional informative bullets pertaining to specific design elements, or simple thoughts and ideas to inspire.

A Guide to the Symbols

Digital Green™ Portfolio

Leveraging Digital technology to achieve Green results. Walk through a kitchen in virtual 3D and explore energy- and water-efficient appliance options.

Efficient Living

A holistic exploration of the Efficient Living theory, concepts and practical applications.

Location

Where we choose to live affects our efficiency; these tips pertain to elements related to site and travel.

Materials & Resources

Information related to the efficient use of materials, recycling, re-using, and re-evaluating the cost of materials from a *Mascord **Efficient Living*** perspective.

Energy

Everything we do involves energy; use these tips and information snippets to decide where and how to save!

Water

Water, water, everywhere, and not a drop to drink. These tips point out where you can reduce your consumption and your utility bill.

Air Quality

The items in our home affect the quality of the air we breathe. Here we highlight the important elements to consider when making choices that affect air quality.

Landscaping

Outdoor living is every bit as important as indoor living. Help is on hand to identify points to consider when planning your garden and landscape.

Digital Green™ Portfolio

Digital Green™ Portfolio
From Whirlpool Corporation
By Mark Johnson, FAIA, CKD, AIBD

From the Printed Page
to the Ideal Home

Whirlpool Corporation is excited to say that the book in your hands is an industry first. We're proud to be the sponsor. Soon you'll discover it's much more than a book. In fact, its very creation represents the coming together of design leaders who share a commitment to both sustainable goals and using technology in bringing home plans to life.

In our view, the more affordable sustainable home designs become, the greater the difference we can make. In other words, as more homes save energy, conserve water and promote good indoor air quality the better for all of us. These diverse and beautiful plans by Alan Mascord Design Associates, Inc., will mean that building green is a reality for the many, not the few.

Following that thought, it can be a challenging process to translate any kind of home plan, green or not, from a dream drawn on paper to an actual dwelling place. That's why Whirlpool Corporation finds technology like Google® SketchUp™ so refreshing. Google® SketchUp™ is a design and visualization tool primarily used by architects and designers. However, its quick and easy features mean you don't have to be an industry professional to use it.

The software, which is on the DVD disc in the back of this book, better enables you to visualize a home before building it—and in 3D! What's more, it also allows you a fast and fun way to explore energy—and water-efficient kitchen and laundry appliance options from the Whirlpool Corporation family of brands, including Jenn-Air®, KitchenAid® and Whirlpool®. How? Keep reading...

Photo courtesy of KitchenAid® Home Appliances

Introducing the Digital Green™ Portfolio

Long before green was so much a part of the popular conscious, Whirlpool Corporation embraced the concept of acting responsibly as a steward of the environment. It was simply the right thing to do, and it still is. Today, we are a leader in harnessing technology to realize sustainable goals, and we have focused special attention in a very logical place. The place where ideas are formed and crucial choices are made: the area of design.

The Digital Green™ Portfolio from Whirlpool Corporation offers cutting-edge, internet-based tools that make it easier to create and visualize projects—right down to choosing appliances. Two components within the portfolio that make this streamlining possible deserve a closer look: the Green Appliance Collection and the Green Home Collection.

The Green Appliance Collection

The energy- and water-efficiency of appliances are certainly major considerations. But what about the efficiency involved in searching through all the appliance options out there, and then making the best choice? The Green Appliance Collection was created to solve this dilemma. So, exactly what is it?

The Green Appliance Collection is a select subcategory of all the virtual appliance models that Whirlpool Corporation has created and placed in a vast library of digital images called the Google® 3D Warehouse. Using Google® SketchUp™ software, anyone can go to the Google® 3D Warehouse and integrate appliances into their plans at the very earliest stages of the design process. The technology works so easily that you can get in on this interactive exploration, too.

As for our total lineup of virtual appliance models, it's the most extensive that any building products manufacturer has placed in the Google® 3D Warehouse. But the Green Appliance Collection narrows our wide array of virtual appliance models down to those offering the most energy and water savings. By searching within the narrowed Green Appliance Collection, you'll be focused in on the most sustainable appliances choices Whirlpool Corporation offers. That means you'll gain a personal savings of time, energy and effort in return.

The Green Home Collection

The Digital Green Portfolio not only contains appliances, but fully realized home designs as well. Aptly named the Green Home Collection—and including plans by Alan Mascord Design Associates, Inc.—it's a virtual gallery of homes showcasing the latest in sustainable practices.

As with the Green Appliance Collection, the Green Home Collection comes alive via Google® SketchUp™ and the Google® 3D Warehouse. The technology allows you to take virtual home tours in 3D. You can see and be inspired by the work of designers who have translated sound, sustainable ideas into comfortable, livable dwellings. If you're in the market for a home plan, you can even find out how to engage the services of the designers themselves.

Mark Johnson, FAIA, CKD, AIBD
Senior manager of Architecture and Design Marketing, Whirlpool Corporation.

Getting Started with Google® SketchUp™

featuring

The DVD included with this book contains the software and files you'll need. If you're not a design professional, don't worry. The steps are easy and the software is user-friendly. Once you're up and running, you can explore many of the kitchen plans in this book in 3D, and even experiment with different appliance models by going to the Google® 3D Warehouse. If you need some training once you've downloaded the software, the tutorials included on the disc will familiarize you with the basics. If you misplace the DVD, just go to sketchup.com to download the free software.

If you master the basics and want to advance your home design skills, check out our free video podcasts. We collaborated with School, creators of the popular series, *The SketchUp Show*, which covers Google SketchUp tips and tricks. To view the five Whirlpool sponsored podcasts, download episodes 20-24 at www.go-2-school.com, or visit the iTunes Store and search for *The SketchUp Show*. (Architects and designers who haven't already discovered Google SketchUp will be glad to know it works on a Mac or PC, and is compatible with most other CAD software.)

No matter whether you're a home-seeker or industry pro, the whole idea is to interact, explore, engage and customize. Not only to bring sustainability down to earth, but also to more closely suit individual wants, needs and preferences.

The Zoned Kitchen.
Where usability drives design.

Mascord Efficient Living offers a wide variety of wonderful home plans with well-thought-out kitchen designs. To gain insight on how these or any other kitchen designs can be tailored to individual preferences, try out the *It's More Than a Kitchen*

Design Tool at www.kitchensforcooks.ca.

This free online tool walks you through a process of discovery, helping you determine your specific lifestyle needs relating to kitchen design. Based on your unique results, it identifies distinct zones within the kitchen and prioritizes the ones that would be most important to you. You'll find solutions tailored to your needs that can be adapted to any size home, including zones for cooking, clean-up, baking, entertaining, kids and more. But why zones?

Developed by KitchenAid® brand of Whirlpool Corporation, the tool is based on research confirming that a majority of homeowners would welcome something other than a one-size-fits all approach: namely, a kitchen designed to accommodate a variety of activities—and in multiple zones.

More than just experimenting with different notions of what's possible, the tool actually helps you identify what you want. In the end, you'll have specific reasons for your design choices and personal knowledge to back up your selection of particular appliances. When building a home, this is great information to have—and to give to your builder, architect or designer.

If you're in the business of building or design, this is great knowledge to act upon. It indicates that the 50+ year-old concept of the kitchen work triangle may not satisfy the wishes of current homebuyers. And, up until now, these wishes may have been difficult for many homebuyers to even communicate in the first place. If you're a builder or designer, why not suggest this tool to your homebuyers or clients? Doing so can help them identify their preferences—and help you respond to them.

When multiple zones are carefully planned for several people working in the kitchen, the result is a more enjoyable experience for everyone. As more square footage and budget dollars are devoted to kitchens than ever before, you owe it to yourself to design the most useable kitchen possible.

Photo courtesy of KitchenAid® Home Appliances

Efficient Living

An Introduction to Efficient Living

As home owners, home builders, and home designers, our individual lifestyles greatly inform our decisions to buy, to build, and to create. In addition, we're becoming increasingly conscious of how these same lifestyles impact our environment. Whether spurred by economic pressures, education, or as a result of world events and first hand experiences—our individual desires to live responsibly are catching up with a collective need to live more efficiently.

We've heard about reducing consumption. We've become more invested in lowering our use of energy. We might have even learned about the onslaught of inventive ways to repurpose our trash. Often the decision to go "green" feels synonymous with the need to sacrifice taste, style, and practicality. Approaching a more efficient way of life frequently comes with a certain degree of trepidation—in approaching sustainability, we wonder, will we have to sacrifice modern conveniences and comforts we otherwise enjoy?

Rest assured, *efficient living* does not mean radically changing your lifestyle. Small steps towards sustainability need not impact your individuality and lifestyle choices. Whether you prefer traditional, contemporary, minimalist, or more eclectic styles—for each individual style there is a way to live more efficiently. In line with your unique style, making small and educated decisions at key points along the buying and building processes can result in a vast improvement in efficiency; you'll also find that sustainable choices result in significant financial savings.

The key is to be educated about the purchases you make. In addition to the initial purchase price, it's important to know how a product works for you, where a product comes from, what you will do with it when you are done, and how much it costs for you to operate.

Armed with this knowledge, you will be able to make smart decisions to improve your financial position, to keep your family and environment safe, and to create a space that best reflects your style. Companies such as Alan Mascord Design Associates and Whirlpool Corporation are responding to environmental concerns by designing homes and products for efficiency and durability, without discounting the ever-present importance of maintaining individual style. While it may seem intuitive, these efficient products and homes really do operate better, last longer, save you money, and are better for the environment. Building an *efficient living* home has never been a smarter, more practical, or more customizable endeavor.

Efficiency, Health, and Sustainability

It's been said that it's not the "bricks and boards" which make a house a home; a house is more deeply colored by its content—the people, the activities, and the sharing of a house are the elements that foster a feeling of home. Yet it is through the decision-laden process of building or choosing a house that a foundation forms—a base from which a sense of home can emerge. From selecting a floor plan to hanging pictures on the wall—ultimately, a home is a culmination of every decision made along the way, both large and small. The combination of these decisions ensures that each home has a unique energy and life of its own, with lasting memories that carry its legacy on; the process of building or choosing a house is where the legacy begins.

The task of making a home is a rich collaboration. Designers, consultants, craftsmen, neighbors, family, and friends make up a large network with an abundant pool of skills to draw upon. John Donne once said that "no man is an island"; nowhere does a statement apply more aptly than to the process of building a house. Working with a capable, knowledgeable, and passionate team is essential in constructing a quality home; it likewise guarantees that you won't feel stranded or overwhelmed in the process.

There are certain universal factors and personal preferences to think about during the creation of your home. "How long will my commute to work be?", "What kind of architectural home styles do I like?", and "What school district do I want to live within?" are a few questions that illuminate what makes a home a highly personal and unique combination of decisions.

Alongside such questions, the 21st century has brought greater environmental and economic concerns that need to be addressed—depleting natural resources, rising energy costs and threatened air quality, among others. To curb the rapidly changing conditions, advancements in the automotive industry are providing options for more fuel efficient (or alternate fuel) cars that are less polluting and can reduce or eliminate the use of depleting natural resources. Better farming practices allow for healthier food options by eliminating the use of environmentally harmful chemicals. Recycling programs are widely accepted and successfully in place—advances in recycling have included the ability to reconstitute more kinds of materials for a greater number of functions than ever before. Despite all of these efforts, the development of our homes is one of the most effective ways to respond to environmental issues.

The construction and operation of homes in the U.S. is one of the largest contributors of environmentally harmful waste and energy consumption. The construction industry's response to these issues is commonly known as *green building*, and is deeply rooted in the idea that everything is holistically connected. This means that all aspects of how your home is built must be considered—including what materials are used in construction, how mechanical systems operate, how your home fits into its community surroundings, and how the house itself affects the lifestyle of the inhabitants.

While researching ways to help our clients build homes using environmentally conscious methods, materials, and products, we strived to uncover answers to many commonly asked home building or buying questions about efficient living—how to create a sustainable lifestyle at a reasonable cost while simultaneously contributing a positively to the environment. On the following pages you will find home design considerations, construction practices, and lifestyle choices that define efficient living—our map to show you how to begin making your new house a home, while protecting your family and the environment.

A few basic themes establish the basis for all of the design considerations, construction practices, and lifestyle choices you will be reading about. These themes include: Efficiency, Health, and Sustainability.

Efficiency

Efficiency is at the heart of many, if not all, of the topics you will read about in this book. According to the American Heritage Dictionary, the definition of *efficient* is: "acting or producing effectively with a minimum of waste, expense, or unnecessary effort." Efficient Living, therefore, seeks effective building techniques, systems and lifestyle choices that result in the smallest amount of waste at the lowest possible expense.

In the following chapters you'll find information on how to consider efficiency and conservation in choosing a home site, building materials, appliances, mechanical systems and landscaping. You'll learn how these choices affect energy, water, and financial efficiency as well as how they can benefit the environment, your community, and your individual lifestyle.

Health

We spend 90% of our time indoors, and a large portion of that time is in our homes. Health, our personal well-being and the well-being of our families, is one of the most important elements to consider when we think about the notion of lifestyle (and constructing a home in line with that lifestyle). Developing a safe, clean, pollutant free environment for our living spaces is essential to maintain good health. Throughout this book you will find information on how to create superior air, water, and light quality.

Sustainability

One way to consider sustainability with regards to home construction and purchasing is by making choices that are durable and long lasting. Some basic examples of sustainable decisions include: incorporating systems that will discourage weather intrusion to the envelope of your house, installing appliances and materials that are well built, and choosing products that have been manufactured using environmentally responsible practices. Throughout this book, you'll discover countless ways to become more sustainable: from energy efficient appliances to the wood used in your home's construction, you'll discover a sustainable choice in nearly every aspect of building and furnishing your home.

Photo courtesy of Steve Mason

Carbon Footprint

With so many sustainable decisions to be made when creating an efficient lifestyle, it might seem difficult to gauge which products, materials, and services are the most environmentally friendly. The *carbon footprint* offers a way to better sort such options by identifying their eco-friendliness.

A carbon footprint is a measurement of the negative impact human actions, products and services have on the environment in terms of the amount of carbon dioxide and other greenhouse gases emitted over their full life cycle. This encompasses your residual impact on the environment. The most common way for you to determine a personal carbon footprint is by analyzing your lifestyle; how much you travel, the efficiency of the vehicles you use, the energy efficiency of your home, and the type of fuel used to operate such vehicles and homes. There are many websites that provide carbon footprint calculators, which typically ask a few simple questions and offer results with comparisons to averages.

The carbon footprint of an individual product is measured through a Life Cycle Assessment (LCA). For more information on LCAs, refer to the *Materials and Resources* section of this book.

Carbon Neutrality

Even after we have taken the steps to live as efficiently as we possibly can, the natural process of using the environment to survive and thrive in the world will invariably leave a mark behind. To minimize our residual impact on the planet, we can think and live with a sense of creative responsibility. Although we unavoidably produce carbon dioxide (CO_2) with our actions, we can promote inventive actions that use up the generated CO_2, thereby negating it. In doing so, we each participate actively in a greater infrastructure, a collective effort to reduce carbon footprints.

Here are 5 key ways you can reduce your Carbon Footprint:

- Build an efficient home with materials that reduce or eliminate CO_2 emissions; consider renewable energy to heat and cool your home.

- Install energy- and water-efficient appliances and mechanical systems in your home.

- Purchase items that have a low carbon footprint from responsible manufacturers.

- Carpool, use mass transit, or plan your trips to reduce driving. Besides homes, gasoline powered automobiles are among the heaviest contributors to carbon dioxide and greenhouse gas emissions.

- Participate in programs that aim to offset carbon dioxide emissions. Many companies today (such as airlines) offer programs to offset your carbon dioxide emissions, which often include donations to renewable energy or tree planting programs.

To view more of this plan, see page 20.

Distinguishing Green

In addition to calculating carbon footprints, there are further ways you can determine the suitability of products for your home. One of these ways is to screen products and services to ensure that they are environmentally safe and eco-friendly, to be certain that when a product or service claims it's green, or efficient, it actually holds up to the highest environmental standards.

Unfortunately, many companies use the term *green* loosely, as a marketing effort to increase their sales. This is termed *green washing*. The practice of green washing brings up the notion of accountability: who really decides which elements are the most sustainable, and furthermore, which company's products are the healthiest and most efficient?

Centrally organized certification programs have been put in place to offer a standard method of measurement. These programs ensure that one item can be compared against a similar item in measurable terms—measurements that can then be assessed by consumers when making purchasing decisions.

To that end, the homes in this collection have been scored based upon their inherent efficiency, to help you consider their individual values before they are built and certified.

Home Certification
More Accessible than Ever Before

A unique benefit of the home plan collection in this book is that Alan Mascord's Efficient Living home designs make it easier and more affordable than ever to earn one of the nationally recognized certifications illustrated below. Imagine lower energy and water bills, a reduced carbon footprint, and a certification that adds value to your home. That is what you can achieve using the *Mascord Efficient Living* instructions, specifications, and certification checklists available for purchase with any of these home plans and the entire plan collection available online.

National Green Building Programs

National certification programs, such as LEED®, NGBS™, and ENERGY STAR, follow standards that are recognized throughout the country. Where local programs are created to suit a single city or state's policy; national programs offer quantifiable certification programs that provide unity and recognition nationwide; they follow stringent procedures outlined by development professionals including the International Code Council (ICC), the American Standards Institute (ANSI), and the American Society of Heating, Refrigerating and Air-conditioning Engineers (ASHRAE) as well as national membership organizations such as the United States Green Building Council (USGBC), or National Association of Home Builders (NAHB).

Local Certification Programs

Local green building programs offer builders and homeowners the opportunity to certify their green built projects with the local community, county, or state in which the building program is located; and allow them to differentiate the certified home from a typical home in the region.

The Value of Verification

Third party verification is a method of quality control used by various certification programs to evaluate and confirm that the installation of efficient features in a home has been completed correctly. A builder or homeowner can use third party verification to distinguish their home from other homes that are self certified by the owner and offer no proof of viability.

ENERGY STAR Homes

ENERGY STAR is not just for appliances or electronics. Though companies like Whirlpool Corporation have taken the lead on achieving the ENERGY STAR for their appliances, it is important to know a home can achieve an ENERGY STAR, too. To earn the ENERGY STAR, a home must meet guidelines for energy efficiency set by the U.S. Environmental Protection Agency. These homes are at least 15% more energy efficient than homes built to the 2004 International Residential Code (IRC).

LEED® for Homes™

The LEED® Rating System is the nationally recognized standard for green building created and managed by the U.S. Green Building Council. LEED® certification recognizes and rewards builders for meeting the highest performance standards, and gives homeowners confidence that their home is durable, healthy, and environmentally friendly. The net cost of owning a LEED® Home is said to be comparable to owning a conventional home.

National Green Building Standard™

The National Green Building Standard™ is the result of a cooperative effort between NAHB and the ICC and is based on NAHB's Model Green Home Building Guidelines, which are the foundation of more than 20 green building programs created by state and local Home Builder Associations throughout the country. The program includes a web-based certification system as well as other tools and resources for builders and certifiers.

Product Verification

When buying an appliance, always remember that it has two price tags: the literal price tag (what you pay to take it home) and the consumption price tag (the costs you will incur for the energy and the water that the appliance uses). With rising utility costs, the latter price tag is quickly becoming the most important of the two.

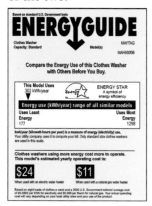

The Energy Guide Label

The energy guide label helps you compare an appliance's energy use to other comparable models by showing you the range (and cost) of energy consumed.

ENERGY STAR

ENERGY STAR qualified appliances incorporate advanced technologies that use 10–50% less energy and water than standard models.

For top performance, premium features, and energy savings—look for ENERGY STAR-approved clothes washers, refrigerators, dishwashers, room air conditioners and dehumidifiers. This mark may appear on the appliance, the packaging or the Energy Guide label.

There are a number of other labels and marks to consider when looking at products. Watch for labels and approvals by the Forest Stewardship Council™ (FSC), which certifies lumber products (including paper), ISO 14001 as a mark of sustainable manufacturing, and endorsements by Greenseal™, an independent, non-profit organization promoting environmentally responsible products and services. Also don't forget the recycling symbol, which gives coded instructions on how to properly limit trash and reuse materials. For additional information, please refer to the *Materials and Resources* section.

Photo courtesy of KitchenAid® Home Appliances

Efficient Lifestyle Choices

Remember that the products we use are also indicators of choices we make. In effect, these choices reflect what we value and the way we live. When examined, the products we choose to purchase (and even the replacement products we seek) speak quite accurately to our individual lifestyles and where our priorities fall.

Consider the products you use in your own everyday life; there may be choices available to save you money as well as choices to be more environmentally responsible. Which choice do you gravitate toward? Keep in mind that environmentally conscious products might initially cost more, but over their entire "useful life" generally cost less (lower operating costs), and are easier to recycle. Additionally, most products designed to be less wasteful and more efficient function just as well as their traditional counterparts. For example,

kitchen towels made from 100% post-consumer recycled paper still absorb liquid as much as non-recycled towels.

To further this particular choice and its impact on the environment, you might take your thinking a step further and ask yourself: Do you need to use paper at all? Would washable cloths be more sustainable? Would using washable cloths save you money on buying paper towels? Is the energy used in producing, shipping and washing those cloths less than producing, shipping, using and recycling paper towels? Do both choices accomplish the same task?

Consideration should also be given to the amount of products consumed. The highest priority should be given to products that will last the longest—items that will be in your life for the longest period of time. Paring down other products not only reduces consumption and the amount of material to recycle, but it also saves money and substantially reduces clutter.

recyclable

Financial Incentives

Local and national tax credits now offer incentives for implementing green and sustainable measures in the construction of your new home. There are also many incentives for energy-efficient appliances and vehicles. In the case of including solar energy equipment, incentives can be as much as 30% of the initial cost of the relevant equipment. When considered alongside the significant savings to be incurred over the life cycle of the products, tax credits can reduce the initial cost of investment and can also guarantee an earlier return in savings. Look online for more information on local and national energy-related tax credits (www.mascordefficientliving.com).

Live Well

Some understand sustainability as a deeply passionate lifestyle conversion. While it certainly can be, the decision to move in a more sustainable direction can also manifest in smaller steps, conscious choices that are complementary to your already considered stylistic ones. Your individual sense of design and space is undoubtedly important when building your home and will govern many of the purchase decisions you make.

When it comes to their impact on the environment, measuring standards such as ENERGY STAR, NGBS™, FSC™ or LEED® offer quantifiable ways of determining the suitability of one product or material over another, and can help clarify which choices are the most cost-conscious and environmentally responsible.

Thankfully, a decision to go green in no way sacrifices your concurrent desire to go fashion forward. You might be surprised to see that the sleek, front-loading washer/drier combo you've been eyeing sports an ENERGY STAR sticker to boot. This is the essence of efficient living: conserving energy, reducing waste, and supporting sustainable products while simultaneously continuing to live well, to your standards, and to your own distinctive tastes.

Terrebonne
Plan G2459

Eco-Conscious Living Can Be Luxurious

Old-World charm meets efficient living in this fantastic French Country home, beautifully crafted by Blazer Development of Portland, Oregon. Showcased in the Street of Dreams, this home exemplifies the sustainability-with-style philosophy. Designed and built to be elegant with a conscience, you'll find as many reasons to catch your breath in this home as you will to breathe its clean air deeply. A durable exterior and healthy interior, along with energy-efficient fixtures and appliances, seamlessly blend with stylish finishes, proof that eco-conscious living can also be luxurious.

Utmost care was taken to protect the site during construction; no dirt was removed from the site, and old-growth trees were preserved while taking advantage of the mountain view. The rear sports area is covered with artificial turf, which carries extremely low maintenance and is pristine to the eye. Beyond its sensory charms, artificial turf eliminates the need for constant watering and mowing, which consumes large quantities of water and energy.

Aesthetic grace and ecological practicality continue to commingle along the home's walkway and outer courtyard. Both elements are paved with permeable surfaces. The cobblestones, engineered from recycled material, allow water to filter naturally into the ground, reducing runoff and erosion tracks. The landscape shares a similar combination of well-appointed visual appeal and environmental benevolence.

On the approach to this home, one would undoubtedly be enthralled by the majesty of the exterior detailing. Beauty is far from being only skin deep here; state of the art technologies blend invisibly with responsible choices throughout.

The roofing material is made from locally produced vertical grain cedar, which is more durable and more sustainable than many other roofing choices the team had. Underneath the stucco exterior, a roll-on waterproof membrane and flexible flashing materials seal the walls which feature efficient,

Photography ©Bob Greenspan

locally produced windows. Exterior details include locally produced faux stone veneers, and also faux shutters constructed from high density foam, protecting investments with reduced maintenance and replacement costs.

Beginning at the front door—a feeling of European warmth and grandeur greets you and your guests in the entryway, where authentic natural plaster walls exude an understated, timeless elegance. These same walls conceal an abundance of energy efficient, moisture resistant, environmentally friendly qualities. Moisture free certified framing and formaldehyde-free loose fill insulation hide beneath the surface. In contrast to traditional sheetrock, the plaster finish is VOC free, resistant to mold, and can significantly reduce your heating and cooling costs through its powerful ability to retain and release heat.

Overhead, the rough-hewn beams in the great room and kitchen complete the impression of the home as a historic, ornately appointed villa. While seemingly dense in material and rich in history, these beams are actually formed from the same high density foam as the exterior shutters. This leaves the beams hollow inside, and more importantly, leaves timber from old-growth forests untouched. In addition, the kitchen's sleek KitchenAid® appliances and elegant interior lighting exceed ENERGY STAR standards.

The indoor environment was of utmost importance to the Blazer Development team, who wisely chose to incorporate measures to protect the air quality of the interior. VOC free paints, natural, sustainable window shades and hard surfaces were used to prevent dust and air pollutants, while a highly efficient HEPA filtered HRV system provides fresh, clean air throughout.

This exquisite home will measure up to your family's environmentally responsible expectations. A testament to the value of protecting our loved ones and, by extension, our environment—this rustic home's conscience makes its stunning architectural beauty all the richer.

Home Facts

Terrebonne
Plan G2459 Price Code **H**

Living Space	Sq Ft
Upper Floor	721
Main Floor	3,631
Total Living Space	**4,352**
Width	100'-6"
Depth	97'-0"
Bedrooms	3*
Bathrooms	3.5

* Number of rooms specifically designed for sleeping quarters. Calculation of bedrooms for certification purposes may be higher.

Efficient Living Rating

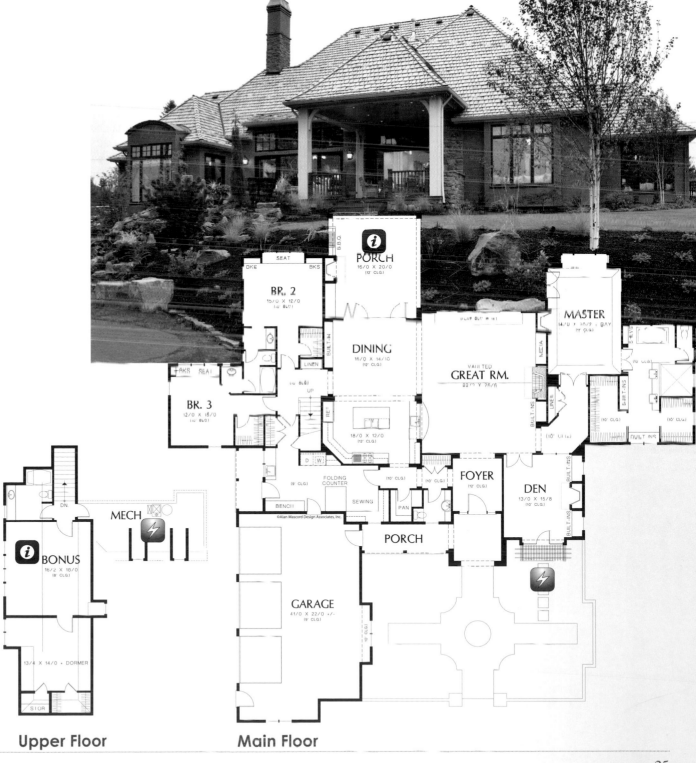

i   Increase living space by taking advantage of nearby outdoor spaces.

⚡   Architecturally interesting shading elements, such as arbors, can provide an attractive feature as well as control heat gain.

i   Bonus rooms provide flexible space for family expansion without the need for remodeling.

⚡   Mechanical equipment operates more efficiently if it is located in a conditioned space, such as this dedicated mechanical room in the attic.

Upper Floor

Main Floor

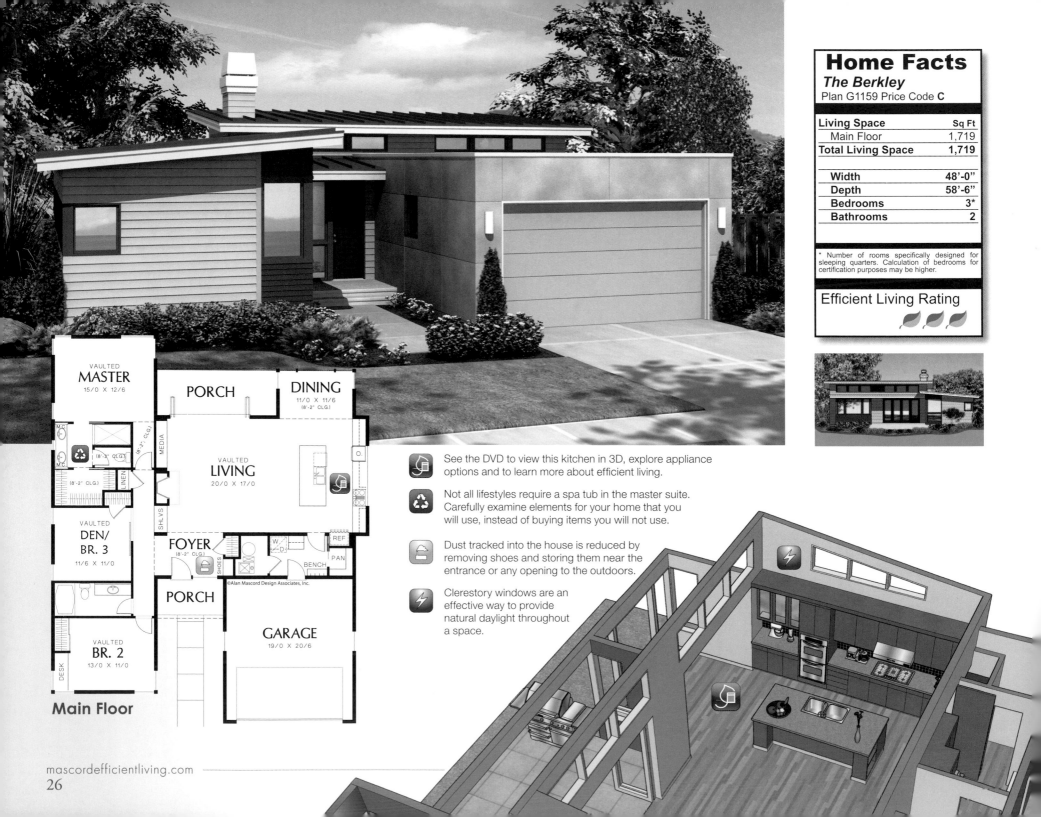

Home Facts

The Berkley
Plan G1159 Price Code **C**

Living Space	Sq Ft
Main Floor	1,719
Total Living Space	**1,719**

Width	48'-0"
Depth	58'-6"
Bedrooms	3*
Bathrooms	2

* Number of rooms specifically designed for sleeping quarters. Calculation of bedrooms for certification purposes may be higher.

Efficient Living Rating

See the DVD to view this kitchen in 3D, explore appliance options and to learn more about efficient living.

Not all lifestyles require a spa tub in the master suite. Carefully examine elements for your home that you will use, instead of buying items you will not use.

Dust tracked into the house is reduced by removing shoes and storing them near the entrance or any opening to the outdoors.

Clerestory windows are an effective way to provide natural daylight throughout a space.

Main Floor

VAULTED
MASTER
15/0 X 12/6

PORCH

DINING
11/0 X 11/6
(8'-2" CLG.)

MEDIA

VAULTED
LIVING
20/0 X 17/0

LINEN

SHLVS

VAULTED
DEN/
BR. 3
11/6 X 11/0

FOYER
(8'-2" CLG.)

SHOES

BENCH

REF
PAN

W/D

VAULTED
BR. 2
13/0 X 11/0

DESK

PORCH

GARAGE
19/0 X 20/6

©Alan Mascord Design Associates, Inc.

Home Facts

Willowdale
Plan G21120 Price Code **C**

Living Space	Sq Ft
Upper Floor	1,032
Main Floor	669
Total Living Space	**1,701**

Width	33'-0"
Depth	46'-0"
Bedrooms	3*
Bathrooms	2

* Number of rooms specifically designed for sleeping quarters. Calculation of bedrooms for certification purposes may be higher.

Efficient Living Rating

BR. 3
10/2 X 11/8

BR. 2
11/8 X 11/8

©Alan Mascord Design Associates, Inc.

GARAGE
19/0 X 22/0

Main Floor

WOOD DECK

VAULTED
LIVING/DINING
22/0 X 17/0

DN.

REF

PANTRY

(9' CLG)   (9' CLG)

VAULTED
MASTER
15/6 X 13/4+

(9' CLG)

Upper Floor

A wall pantry uses less space than a walk-in pantry and still provides comparable storage.

This open floor plan with combined living and dining areas feels spacious while remaining efficient.

Creative use of built-ins can make smaller spaces more efficient.

Home Facts

The Penrod
Plan G22163 Price Code E

Living Space	Sq Ft
Upper Floor	1,525
Main Floor	1,205
Total Living Space	**2,730**

Width	30'-0"
Depth	68'-0"
Bedrooms	4*
Bathrooms	3

*Number of rooms specifically designed for sleeping quarters. Calculation of bedrooms for certification purposes may be higher.

Efficient Living Rating

See the DVD to view this kitchen in 3D, explore appliance options and to learn more about efficient living.

Shared bathroom amenities reduce the number of fixtures to purchase, plumb, and power.

A single door for a 3-car garage can reduce material usage, saving in door and mechanical equipment costs.

Consider using a commercial car wash that uses recycled water. If you choose to wash your car at home, park it on the grass to do so.

Although only 7 x 7, this study is an efficient, functional area.

©Alan Mascord Design Associates, Inc.

VAULTED
MASTER BR
16/0 X 14/6

BR. 2
12/6 X 11/0 +/-
(9' CLG.)

BR. 3
12/6 X 10/0 +/-
(9' CLG.)

SPA

STUDY
7/0 X 7/0
(10'-6" CLG.)

VAULTED
GAME RM.
15/0 X 11/0

Upper Floor

GREAT RM.
16/0 X 16/0
(10'-6" CLG.)

DEN/BR.4
10/6 X 11/0
(9' CLG.)

DINING
16/0 X 11/0
(10'-6" CLG.)

3RD BAY
10/6 X 16/0

12/0 X 14/0
(9' CLG.)

GARAGE
19/0 X 21/6

©Alan Mascord Design Associates, Inc.

Main Floor

Home Facts

Camden
Plan G2261H Price Code **E**

Living Space	Sq Ft
Upper Floor	1,181
Main Floor	1,319
Total Living Space	**2,500**
Bonus Room	+371
Width	**60'-0"**
Depth	**42'-0"**
Bedrooms	**4***
Bathrooms	**2.5**

* Number of rooms specifically designed for sleeping quarters. Calculation of bedrooms for certification purposes may be higher.

Efficient Living Rating

This garage can be removed if it is not needed or to reduce costs.

Simple, efficient foundation footprints require less labor to construct and can save material.

Retrofit wasteful faucets with aerators with flow restrictors.

Raise the lawn mower blade to at least 3". Longer blades of grass shade the root system and prevent evaporation more efficiently than a short cut lawn.

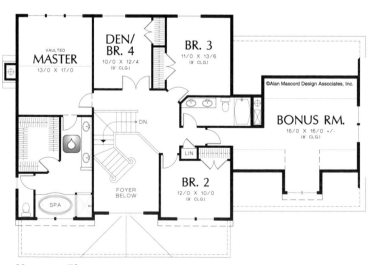

Main Floor

FAMILY
13/0 X 17/0
(9' CLG.)

NOOK
8/0 X 13/0
(9' CLG.)

10/0 X 14/2
(9' CLG.)

DESK

NICHE

REF PAN

BUTLER'S PANTRY

GARAGE
21/6 X 28/0

LIVING
13/0 X 16/6
(9' CLG.)

UP

2 STORY
FOYER

DINING
12/0 X 11/0
(9' CLG.)

©Alan Mascord Design Associates, Inc.

Upper Floor

VAULTED
MASTER
13/0 X 17/0

DEN/
BR. 4
10/0 X 12/4
(9' CLG.)

BR. 3
11/0 X 13/6
(9' CLG.)

©Alan Mascord Design Associates, Inc.

BONUS RM.
16/0 X 16/0 +/-
(8' CLG.)

DN.

LIN

FOYER
BELOW

SPA

BR. 2
12/0 X 10/0
(9' CLG.)

Home Facts

The Nichols
Plan G22164 Price Code **D**

Living Space	Sq Ft
Upper Floor	1,248
Main Floor	863
Total Living Space	**2,111**

Width	27'-0"
Depth	69'-6"
Bedrooms	3*
Bathrooms	2.5

* Number of rooms specifically designed for sleeping quarters. Calculation of bedrooms for certification purposes may be higher.

Efficient Living Rating

 See the DVD to view the home in 3D, explore appliance options, and to learn more about efficient living.

 Window shades provide a method of controlling solar heat gain in the summer while allowing warmth in the winter.

 A rear loading garage promotes access to pedestrian oriented neighborhoods.

 Natural daylight is allowed to penetrate inner areas by positioning windows appropriately.

Main Floor

Upper Floor

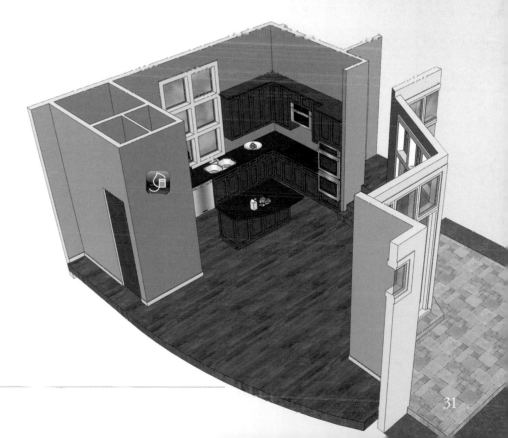

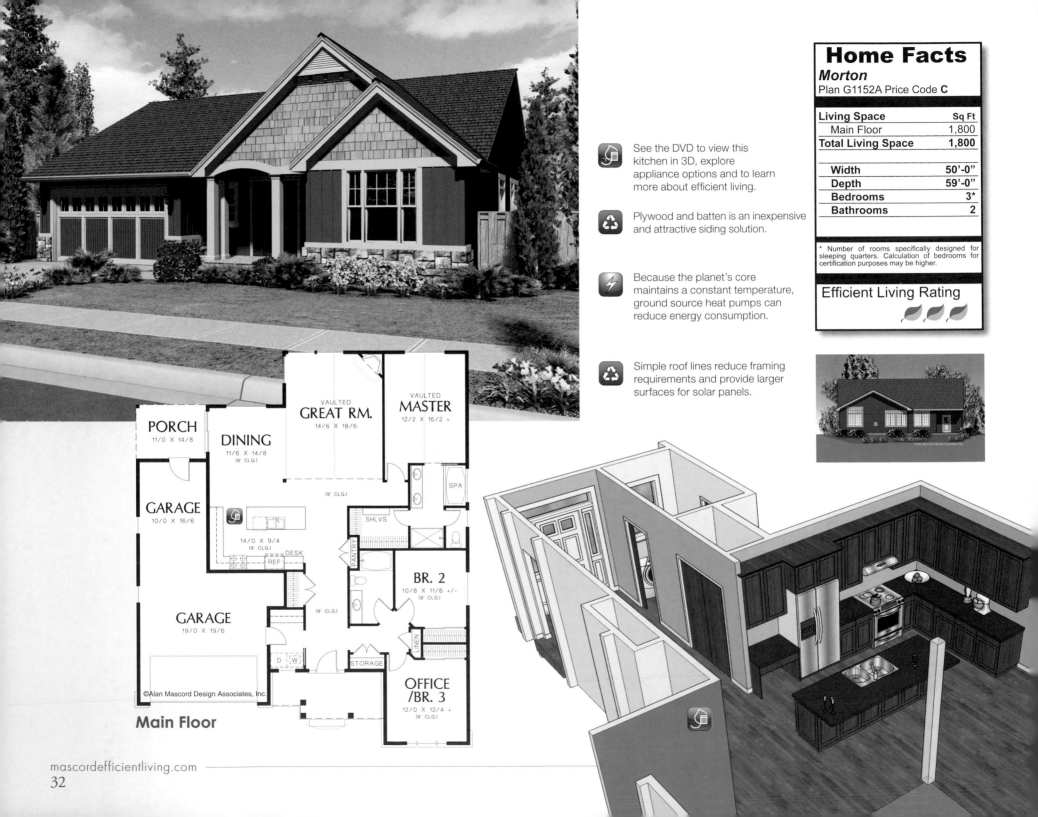

Home Facts

Morton

Plan G1152A Price Code **C**

Living Space	Sq Ft
Main Floor	1,800
Total Living Space	**1,800**

Width	50'-0"
Depth	59'-0"
Bedrooms	3*
Bathrooms	2

* Number of rooms specifically designed for sleeping quarters. Calculation of bedrooms for certification purposes may be higher.

Efficient Living Rating

See the DVD to view this kitchen in 3D, explore appliance options and to learn more about efficient living.

Plywood and batten is an inexpensive and attractive siding solution.

Because the planet's core maintains a constant temperature, ground source heat pumps can reduce energy consumption.

Simple roof lines reduce framing requirements and provide larger surfaces for solar panels.

Main Floor

PORCH
11/0 X 14/8

DINING
11/6 X 14/8
(9' CLG.)

VAULTED
GREAT RM.
14/6 X 18/6

VAULTED
MASTER
12/2 X 16/2 +

SPA

GARAGE
10/0 X 16/6

(9' CLG.)

14/0 X 9/4
(9' CLG.)

SHLVS

DESK

REF

PANTRY

BR. 2
10/8 X 11/6 +/-
(9' CLG.)

GARAGE
19/0 X 19/6

(9' CLG.)

D W

LINEN

STORAGE

OFFICE
/BR. 3
12/0 X 12/4 +
(9' CLG.)

©Alan Mascord Design Associates, Inc.

Home Facts

Elsie
Plan G21116A Price Code **C**

Living Space	Sq Ft
Upper Floor	757
Main Floor	932
Total Living Space	**1,689**

Width	22'-0"
Depth	48'-0"
Bedrooms	3*
Bathrooms	2.5

* Number of rooms specifically designed for sleeping quarters. Calculation of bedrooms for certification purposes may be higher.

Efficient Living Rating

BR. 2
10/4 X 11/8
(9' CLG.)

BR. 3
10/4 X 11/8
(9' CLG.)

DN.

MASTER
12/0 X 13/2
(9' CLG.)

Upper Floor

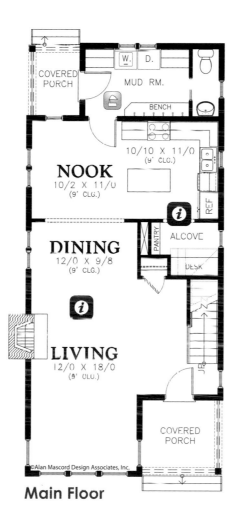

COVERED PORCH

MUD RM.

W. D.

BENCH

10/10 X 11/0
(9' CLG.)

NOOK
10/2 X 11/0
(9' CLG.)

REF

PANTRY

ALCOVE

DINING
12/0 X 9/8
(9' CLG.)

DESK

LIVING
12/0 X 18/0
(9' CLG.)

COVERED PORCH

©Alan Mascord Design Associates, Inc.

Main Floor

 Instead of having a full office, which requires more space, this plan takes advantage of the area underneath the stairs for a functional work space.

 Light on two adjacent sides of a room provides an even level of natural light, reducing the need for additional artificial light.

Space allocated to movement, such as hallways and corridors, is reduced in this efficient plan, allowing room for more livable space.

This plan features a space saving and functional half bath and mudroom.

Home Facts

Hudson

Plan G21112 Price Code **C**

Living Space	Sq Ft
Upper Floor	595
Main Floor	1,130
Total Living Space	**1,725**

Width	29'-0"
Depth	57'-0"
Bedrooms	3*
Bathrooms	2.5

* Number of rooms specifically designed for sleeping quarters. Calculation of bedrooms for certification purposes may be higher.

Efficient Living Rating

Storage pantries can be used to store bulk items, reducing shopping trips and packaging materials associated with purchasing smaller quantities frequently.

Consider a shower instead of a bath. The amount of water needed to fill a tub varies, but on average it is less than 10 gallons for a shower.

ENERGY STAR dishwashers actually use less water than washing dishes by hand.

This plan takes advantage of otherwise wasted space under the stairs for a coat closet.

MASTER 12/0 X 14/0 (12' CLG.)

LIVING 15/8 X 14/0 (12' CLG.)

DINING 14/6 X 10/0 (12' CLG.)

W/D

LIN

(9' CLG.)

(9' CLG.)

UP

PAN

REF

(2 STORY)

(9' CLG.)

GARAGE 19/0 X 19/0

©Alan Mascord Design Associates, Inc.

Main Floor

OPEN TO BELOW

DN.

BR. 3/OFFICE 16/10 X 10/10

BUILT-INS LINEN

MASTER 2 12/6 X 14/0

Upper Floor

Home Facts

The Norwood
Plan G22153 Price Code **D**

Living Space	Sq Ft
Upper Floor	1,073
Main Floor	1,205
Total Living Space	**2,278**

Width	42'-0"
Depth	46'-6"
Bedrooms	3*
Bathrooms	2.5

* Number of rooms specifically designed for sleeping quarters. Calculation of bedrooms for certification purposes may be higher.

Efficient Living Rating

Slow release herbicides and fertilizers can help reduce site contamination and the need for recurrent applications.

Make sure your home is well insulated. Ceiling insulation is most important for year round comfort. Also consider upgrading the wall and floor insulation.

Rather than installing and operating two fireplaces, this dual-sided fireplace functions in two rooms.

Main Floor

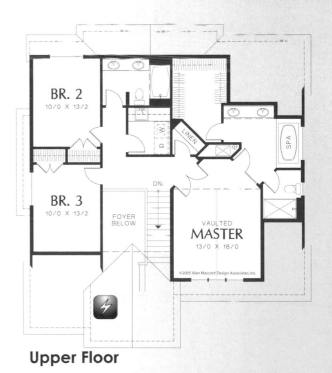

Upper Floor

 See the DVD to view this kitchen in 3D, explore appliance options and to learn more about efficient living.

 Pervious materials used for surfaces such as drive and walkways allow rainfall to percolate into the ground.

 Covered porches offer stylish ways to shade windows to control summer sun.

 This plan takes advantage of otherwise unusable space in the attic for storage.

Home Facts
Northbrook
Plan G22122Q Price Code **E**

Living Space	Sq Ft
Upper Floor	675
Main Floor	1,838
Total Living Space	**2,513**
Bonus Room	+440
Width	56'-0"
Depth	62'-0"
Bedrooms	4*
Bathrooms	2.5

* Number of rooms specifically designed for sleeping quarters. Calculation of bedrooms for certification purposes may be higher.

Efficient Living Rating

Upper Floor

Main Floor

Home Facts

Juniper

Plan G21118B Price Code **B**

Living Space	Sq Ft
Upper Floor	661
Main Floor	832
Total Living Space	**1,493**
Width	22'-0"
Depth	40'-0"
Bedrooms	3*
Bathrooms	2.5

* Number of rooms specifically designed for sleeping quarters. Calculation of bedrooms for certification purposes may be higher.

Efficient Living Rating

Detached garage plan available.

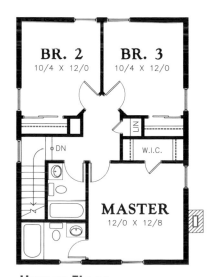

Upper Floor

BR. 2
10/4 X 12/0

BR. 3
10/4 X 12/0

MASTER
12/0 X 12/8

W.I.C.

LIN.

DN

Main Floor

MUDROOM

BENCH

DINING
10/2 X 11/7
(9' CLG.)

10/10 X 11/7
(9' CLG.)

REF

DN FOR BSMT

PAN

DESK

LIVING
17/6 X 12/9
(9' CLG.)

COVERED PORCH

©Alan Mascord Design Associates, Inc.

Unplug battery chargers when the batteries are fully charged or not in use.

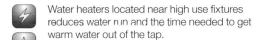
Water heaters located near high use fixtures reduces water run and the time needed to get warm water out of the tap.

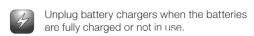
Finishing wood flooring with OS Hardwood Oil, an all plant oil based finish, provides a lasting finish free from VOC's.

Preserving existing trees and foliage can increase the value of your property as well as maintain the environment.

Home Facts

Osprey
Plan G21115 Price Code **C**

Living Space	Sq Ft
Upper Floor	778
Main Floor	1,096
Total Living Space	**1,874**

Width	28'-0"
Depth	43'-0"
Bedrooms	2*
Bathrooms	2

* Number of rooms specifically designed for sleeping quarters. Calculation of bedrooms for certification purposes may be higher.

Efficient Living Rating

Detached garage plan available

Note: Photographed home may have been modified to suit homeowner's preference.

 Try not to put water down the drain that can be used for watering plants or cleaning.

 Use task lighting instead of lighting an entire room. Only focus light where it is needed. For example, use fluorescent under-cabinet lights in the kitchen.

 Don't over water your lawn. As a general rule, lawns only need watering once inch per week.

MASTER
11/3 X 13/1
(9' CLG.)

15/4 X 9/4
(9' CLG.)

DINING
13/0 X 11/11
(9' CLG.)

LIVING
15/4 X 12/11
(9' CLG.)

W. D. PAN
MUDROOM
BENCH
REF
UP
COVERED PORCH

©Alan Mascord Design Associates, Inc.

Main Floor

BR. 2
10/5 X 15/10
(9' CLG.)

BR. 3
10/5 X 15/10
(9' CLG.)

DESK
DN

MEDIA
15/7 X 9/5
(9' CLG.)

Upper Floor

Home Facts

The Galen
Plan G1231 Price Code **D**

Living Space	Sq Ft
Main Floor	2,001
Total Living Space	**2,001**

Width	60'-0"
Depth	50'-0"
Bedrooms	3 *
Bathrooms	2

* Number of rooms specifically designed for sleeping quarters. Calculation of bedrooms for certification purposes may be higher.

Efficient Living Rating

See the DVD to view this kitchen in 3D, explore appliance options and to learn more about efficient living.

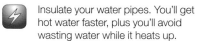
Insulate your water pipes. You'll get hot water faster, plus you'll avoid wasting water while it heats up.

This tandem garage reduces the width needed to house three cars, and offers flexible space for expansion at a later date.

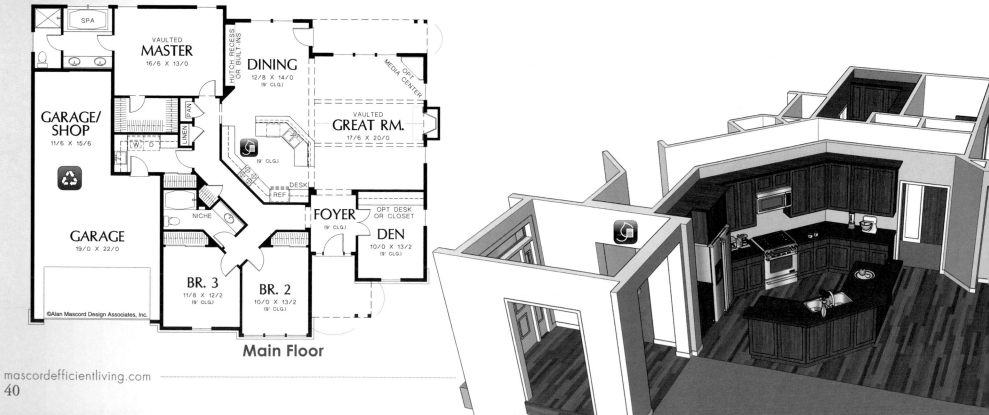

SPA

VAULTED
MASTER
16/6 X 13/0

HUTCH RECESS OR BUILT-INS

DINING
12/8 X 14/0
(9' CLG.)

OPT MEDIA CENTER

VAULTED
GREAT RM.
17/6 X 20/0

GARAGE/
SHOP
11/6 X 15/6

PAN

LINEN

W D

(9' CLG.)

DESK

REF

FOYER
(9' CLG.)

OPT DESK
OR CLOSET

NICHE

GARAGE
19/0 X 22/0

DEN
10/0 X 13/2
(9' CLG.)

BR. 3
11/8 X 12/2
(9' CLG.)

BR. 2
10/0 X 13/2
(9' CLG.)

©Alan Mascord Design Associates, Inc.

Main Floor

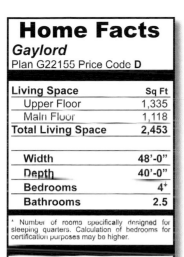

Upper Floor

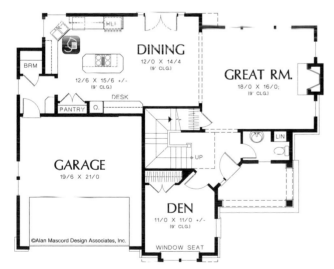

Main Floor

 See the DVD to view the home in 3D, explore appliance options, and to learn more about Efficient Living.

Use 4 ft. fluorescent lights for work rooms, garages, and laundry areas.

Street trees mature over time and can help reduce regional heat island effects by shading roadways

Do not water the street or driveway. Carefully position sprinklers so that water only lands on areas that need it.

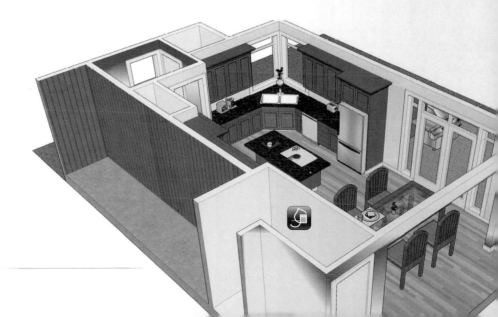

Location

Location, Location, Location

As the old adage suggests, location is everything. The physical place we choose for our homes has a profound affect on our lifestyle. Neighborhoods each have their own unique flavor and daily pulse, down to the specific street, block, and plot of land on which a house sits. Because our lives are deeply intertwined with the neighborhoods we live in, each location presents its own unique sensibilities and challenges, regardless of whether we live an urban, rural, or suburban lifestyle.

Resources available in a particular neighborhood will determine how efficient your lifestyle will be before you even break ground. Distances to local amenities such as schools and stores are as important as having utilities at your site. Extra distance means extra time, energy and emissions during the commute. When choosing a location, the closer to amenities your home is, the more efficient you are likely to be. The right choice of location can be extremely cost effective, and most lucrative to both yourself and the environment.

After choosing an appropriate geographical location for your home, the site you pick has further potential to improve your efficiency. Beyond the more widely understood concerns (such as size and slope of the lot, upkeep, actual usability of space, and possible building setbacks), there are a few other elements to consider. The location of the sun, natural topography and existing plant life all play important roles when planning to use your site to its fullest potential. When choosing a *Mascord Efficient Living* plan, it's wise to consider how the home will work with all the elements discussed in this section.

Build for Your Climate Zone and Local Environment

The local weather conditions surrounding your home profoundly affect the construction practices recommended for your area. Temperature, humidity, air pressure and wind exposure all need to be considered when constructing your home. Determine how local weather patterns and temperature changes will affect the durability of your home. The department of Energy has developed a map (viewable at www.epa.gov) which separates the USA into different Climate Zones. Each zone has unique recommendations for such things as window efficiency, thermal performance, and moisture prevention measures. In addition to considering the weather, a suitable location should certainly avoid sensitive areas such as wetlands and floodplains.

Respecting The Site

It is highly important to respect the environment that is already present at your home site. If possible, try to work with existing topography, plants, and views. Trees are valuable; work around old growth trees to keep them as part of your landscape. Old-growth trees add to the resale value of your home; they help the landscape mature and provide your home shade during summer months, which reduces energy costs.

When it comes to landscaping, remember to touch the earth lightly, rather than clearing the landscape and re-landscaping with non-native plants. Doing so will help with erosion control, preserve desirable landscape features, and protect local eco-systems. Clearing a hillside of vegetation can destabilize the land and can lead to landslides and excessive rainwater run-off during heavy downpours. The geologic composition of many hills often means there are non-permeable clay layers that prevent layers above from draining. Water can build up above the clay layer to a point where the ground is saturated, and the top layers can literally slide off the clay. It's best not to clear your home site as the natural vegetation in the top layers can hold the hillside together and aid in water retention.

Along with their natural ability to prevent erosion, trees clean the air around your home. They do so by processing carbon dioxide during photosynthesis, whereby light and carbon dioxide are converted to glucose and oxygen.

Solar Orientation

Optimal solar orientation involves placing your home to take full advantage of natural daylight and the sun's power. This entails more than getting light in your home: it harnesses natural energy. That means minimizing your heating and cooling requirements as well as limiting your need to have lights on throughout the day. Additionally, you might use non-mechanical elements in your home to heat and cool your living space: this is called passive solar design. The effect passive solar design has on your energy consumption and the environment, however, is far from being passive.

Positioning your home for passive solar design means having your windows in the best location with respect to the sun. Ideally, windows and shading devices should reduce the amount of sun rays they let in during the summer while also permitting the highest possible amount during the winter. The Sun's rays emit solar radiation, which creates heat for your home.

To employ the sun most optimally, your home should be positioned along an east west axis with the maximum amount of windows on the south side. In the northern hemisphere, the sun moves from east to west across the sky at a high angle in the summer, and low in the winter. The south facing windows will have the most exposure to sunlight allowing you to take advantage of the sun's energy to heat and light your home. To prevent excessive exposure during summer, the south side of your home can be easily protected from the sun with appropriate overhangs or shading elements.

Reducing the amount of windows on the east and west side of the house will minimize exposure at dawn and sunset, when windows are more difficult to shade due to the lower angle of the sun. If needed, east and west sides can be protected from the sun with trees and shrubbery, or with other shading elements.

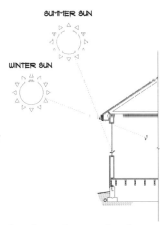

Southern Sun angles change with the season.

When thinking about the orientation of your home on your site, maximizing south facing roof planes will allow for the addition of roof top systems to harness the sun's energy for free power.

An existing tree and top soil preservation plan, along with stockpiled dirt protection measures, were implemented at this environmentally responsible Seabrook development in Washington.

Minimize your commute

Living in a remote location will also mean a long commute to work, school, or the store. Do you really want to sit in traffic on a hot summer night?

Smart Growth

The philosophy behind some environmentally friendly developments is to live close to where you work, rest and play. If you live locally to everything you need, you'll be able to get from point A to B quickly, economically, and possibly without a car. With such advantages in mind, consider building in a development that will include all the amenities you will need. Look for developments that are compact and naturally form close-knit communities where amenities are within walking distance, you can get to know your neighbors, and your children can play safely. Density fosters safety, good physical health and a higher quality of life.

There are a number of items typically included in a well-planned development. At the center of the community is often an activity center—this is typically a plaza, square or green space (or sometimes a busy or noteworthy intersection). Special attention is paid to creating quality public spaces, including sidewalks and pathways, parks, and public buildings, which help create a community identity. There are commonly places to work—within and adjacent to the residential neighborhood, including stores, office buildings, and production facilities. In a well-planned development, take a look at the stores themselves. They should be sufficiently varied to meet common household needs, with the presence of outlets like convenience stores, gyms, post offices, banks, groceries, etc. Schools should be close enough so that most children can walk from their homes.

Thoroughfares shaded by rows of trees and designed to slow traffic create an environment suitable for pedestrians and bicyclists. A well-planned network of pathways can reduce distances between residences and businesses for pedestrians.

Enjoying the outdoors in a close knit community at Seabrook, Washington.

Photo courtesy of Steve Mason

Urban Growth / Infill

An infill lot is a space in a metropolitan area that has previously been unused or abandoned. Vacant land for new construction can be found in established communities. Infill lots can vary in size and be as small as 2,500 square feet or less. Larger parcels of land in existing neighborhoods can also be subdivided to increase density. Consult your local building department for information and opportunities.

Infill lots often have access to existing utilities nearby: electric, gas, water and sewer. They are also likely to be near existing retail outlets, public transport, and other needed amenities – adding to your efficiency.

Transit Options

When choosing a home site consider the costs you are likely to incur as a result of daily commuting and examine the options you have to reduce those costs. What exactly are the options you have when it comes to traveling around your local area? If you cannot live within walking or cycling distance of the place you work, you may be able to car pool, travel by bus, rail, or streetcar. Many municipalities offer a well-budgeted combination of these services. Taking advantage of such services on a consistent basis reduces energy use, carbon emissions and costs related to personal transportation.

47

Seabrook, Washington

In Harmony with Nature

How one Washington coastal town was developed to co-exist beautifully and sustainably with its natural surroundings

On a beautiful stretch of the Washington coast lies a small town that was built on sustainable ideals. The vision? To create an environmentally responsible community that would endure for generations to come. Seabrook Land Development planned the town with sustainable practices in mind from the very start. Through a combined effort to preserve the area's natural resources and to minimize its long-term environmental impact, the Seabrook community was born.

The central philosophy of new urbanism, a community living in harmony with nature, is evident throughout the town; from the network of pathways paved with eco-friendly materials like reclaimed crushed oyster shell and cedar mulch, to the lack of cars on the streets. The town of Seabrook was planned specifically to encourage walking and cycling, with all stores and restaurants accessible within a five-minute walk from home. With the exception of community areas, grass lawns are excluded - reducing community water usage and pollutants caused by pesticides and gas mowers.

Homes are constructed out of respect for their natural surroundings to create as little environmental impact as possible, preserving existing topsoil, vegetation and trees. Any disturbed vegetation is either reclaimed and replanted in another part of the community or replaced with native plants grown in an on-site nursery. One common trench, containing the electric, gas, cable, television and telephone lines, runs beneath all the homes in Seabrook. By digging the trench all at once, construction was less disruptive and more efficient, saving resources and preserving natural areas.

Left: Built to harness the qualities of a well-established neighborhood of the past, Seabrook offers modern day conveniences throughout the tight-knit community.

From the plumbing to the rooftops, the homes are designed to be energy efficient and environmentally responsible, employing eco-friendly alternatives and making use of available materials that would otherwise be discarded. The homes' outer shells and inner ducts are carefully sealed to prevent air from entering or escaping, lowering energy costs. The designs also feature whole-house-ventilation systems that regularly circulate stale air out of the homes and brings fresh air inside. The homes are painted and caulked with substances that contain low amounts of volatile organic compounds (VOCs)—chemicals released during construction and throughout their lifetime –improving indoor air quality over homes using traditional paints and sealers. Lighting fixtures are ENERGY STAR rated, reducing energy usage by 75%, and the homes' dishwashers and water heaters have high energy efficiency rankings.

On site, reclaimed and salvaged cedar trees are transformed by local mills into shingles and siding for Seabrook homes. Composite wood board made from recycled chips and scraps is also used, reducing the demand on forest timber. Floors are laid using salvaged Doug Fir planks that are finished with plant-based oil, free of harmful VOCs. Medium-Density Fiberboard, composed of wood fiber from sawmill waste, is chosen for the homes' walls. Owners can be proud of their homes' low environmental impact, from building materials to energy usage.

Outside, residents are encouraged to interact with their beautiful surroundings. They can simply sit on the front porch and enjoy the view, or gather at the central amphitheater and playground. They can also view the rugged coastline bordered by towering spruce by walking down one of the many trails to the beach. For the community of Seabrook and its residents, the future looks very green indeed.

Home Facts

Ashville
Plan G21116B Price Code **C**

Living Space	Sq Ft
Upper Floor	757
Main Floor	932
Total Living Space	**1,689**
Width	22'-0"
Depth	48'-0"
Bedrooms	3*
Bathrooms	2 Full 2 Half

* Number of rooms specifically designed for sleeping quarters. Calculation of bedrooms for certification purposes may be higher.

Efficient Living Rating

Detached garage plan available.

Please note: Photographed home may have been modified to suit homeowner's preference. The home pictured here was built without the mudroom.

Whenever possible, choose roofing and siding materials that contain a high content of recycled material and/or are recyclable themselves.

Combine trips to the store to reduce mileage and emissions. When choosing a property, consider your proximity to conveniences such as the grocery store and gas stations to avoid having to drive excess distances when running errands.

Main Floor

COVERED PORCH

MUD RM.

W. D.

BENCH

12/1 X 11/8 (9' CLG.)

NOOK 9/0 X 11/0 (9' CLG.)

REF

PAN

DINING 12/0 X 8/4 (9' CLG.)

LIVING 12/0 X 18/7 (9' CLG.)

UP

COVERED PORCH

©Alan Mascord Design Associates, Inc.

Upper Floor

BR. 2 10/4 X 11/8 (9' CLG.)

BR. 3 10/4 X 11/8 (9' CLG.)

DN

MASTER 12/0 X 13/2 (9' CLG.)

COVERED PORCH

Home Facts

Wandell

Plan G1143 Price Code **C**

Living Space	Sq Ft
Main Floor	1,230
Lower Floor	769
Total Living Space	**1,999**

Width	40'-0"
Depth	53'-0"
Bedrooms	3*
Bathrooms	2.5

* Number of rooms specifically designed for sleeping quarters. Calculation of bedrooms for certification purposes may be higher.

Efficient Living Rating

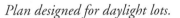

Plan designed for daylight lots.

 To save energy, make sure the seals around your freezer doors are sealed.

Consider light wall colors to minimize the need for artificial lighting.

 Use hose washers between spigots and hoses to eliminate leaks.

Lower Floor

BR. 2
10/6 X 12/8

BR. 3
10/8 X 11/0

REC. RM.
14/10 X 12/8

CRAWLSPACE

UP

STORAGE

Main Floor

DECK

VAULTED
MASTER
16/2 X 13/0

SCISSOR VAULTED
LIVING/DINING
15/2 X 20/2

LIN.

D. W.

PAN.

GARAGE
19/6 X 20/0

REF

DN.

DEN
11/0 X 10/0
(10' CLG.)

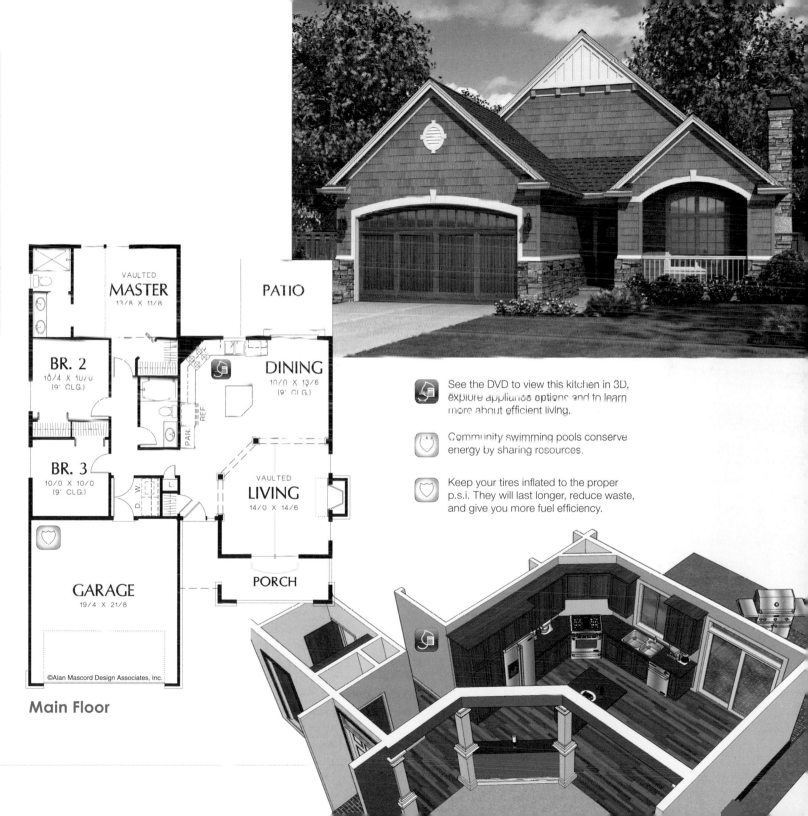

Home Facts

Cypress
Plan G1111AC Price Code **B**

Living Space	Sq Ft
Main Floor	1,275
Total Living Space	**1,275**

Width	40'-0"
Depth	58'-0"
Bedrooms	3*
Bathrooms	2

* Number of rooms specifically designed for sleeping quarters. Calculation of bedrooms for certification purposes may be higher.

Efficient Living Rating

Main Floor

VAULTED
MASTER
13/8 X 11/8

PATIO

BR. 2
10/4 X 10/0
(9' CLG.)

DINING
10/0 X 13/6
(9' CLG.)

BR. 3
10/0 X 10/0
(9' CLG.)

VAULTED
LIVING
14/0 X 14/6

GARAGE
19/4 X 21/8

PORCH

PAN.

REF.

D. W.

©Alan Mascord Design Associates, Inc.

See the DVD to view this kitchen in 3D, explore appliance options and to learn more about efficient living.

Community swimming pools conserve energy by sharing resources.

Keep your tires inflated to the proper p.s.i. They will last longer, reduce waste, and give you more fuel efficiency.

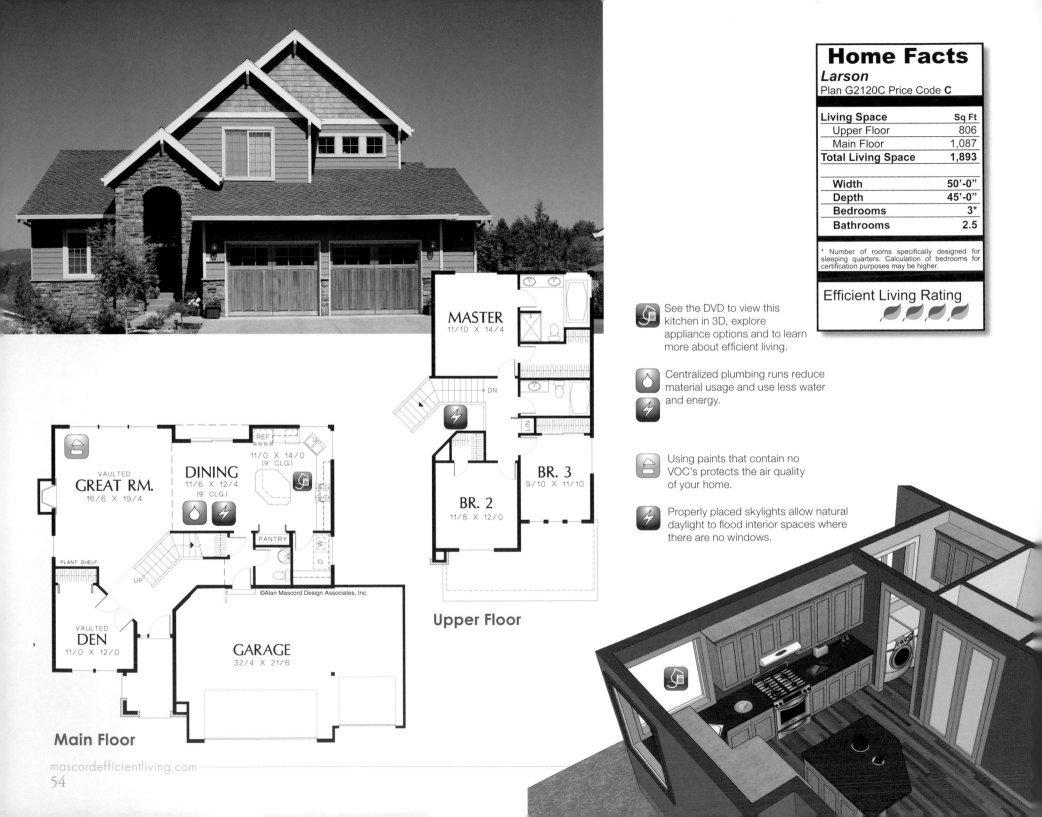

Home Facts

Larson
Plan G2120C Price Code **C**

Living Space	Sq Ft
Upper Floor	806
Main Floor	1,087
Total Living Space	**1,893**

Width	50'-0"
Depth	45'-0"
Bedrooms	3*
Bathrooms	2.5

* Number of rooms specifically designed for sleeping quarters. Calculation of bedrooms for certification purposes may be higher.

Efficient Living Rating

See the DVD to view this kitchen in 3D, explore appliance options and to learn more about efficient living.

Centralized plumbing runs reduce material usage and use less water and energy.

Using paints that contain no VOC's protects the air quality of your home.

Properly placed skylights allow natural daylight to flood interior spaces where there are no windows.

MASTER
11/10 X 14/4

BR. 3
9/10 X 11/10

BR. 2
11/8 X 12/0

DN

LIN

Upper Floor

VAULTED
GREAT RM.
16/6 X 19/4

DINING
11/6 X 12/4
(9' CLG.)

REF

11/0 X 14/0
(9' CLG.)

PANTRY

PLANT SHELF

UP

VAULTED
DEN
11/0 X 12/0

GARAGE
32/4 X 21/6

©Alan Mascord Design Associates, Inc.

Main Floor

Home Facts

Dearborn
Plan G22151A Price Code **E**

Living Space	Sq Ft
Upper Floor	1,390
Main Floor	1,216
Total Living Space	**2,606**

Width	50'-0"
Depth	42'-0"
Bedrooms	4*
Bathrooms	2.5

* Number of rooms specifically designed for sleeping quarters. Calculation of bedrooms for certification purposes may be higher.

Efficient Living Rating

 See the DVD to view this kitchen in 3D, explore appliance options and to learn more about efficient living.

 Buy reusable or refillable products to minimize waste from packaging.

 Water lawns during early morning or late evening when temperatures are lowest to reduce losses from evaporation.

Main Floor

SHOP 10/0 X 11/6

GARAGE 19/6 X 20/6

NOOK 11/0 X 11/0 (9' CLG.)

GREAT RM. 18/0 X 18/10 (9' CLG.)

11/0 X 11/8 +/- (9' CLG.)

OPTIONAL MEDIA CNTR.

DINING 11/6 X 12/10 (9' CLG.)

TWO STORY FOYER

VAULTED DEN 10/0 X 11/2

PAN. REF.

UP

©Alan Mascord Design Associates, Inc

Upper Floor

BR. 4 11/0 X 12/2 (9' CLG.)

SPA

MASTER 14/0 X 18/10 (9' CLG.)

LINEN

SHLVS.

NICHE

(9' CLG.)

BR. 3 16/0 X 15/2 +/- (9' CLG.)

(9' CLG.)

LIN

DN

BR. 2 11/0 X 15/10 +/- (9' CLG.)

FOYER BELOW

©Alan Mascord Design Associates, Inc

Home Facts
Cabot
Plan G22171B Price Code **D**

Living Space	Sq Ft
Upper Floor	801
Main Floor	941
Total Living Space	**2,224**
vBonus Room	+482
Width	**24'-0"**
Depth	**43'-0"**
Bedrooms	**3***
Bathrooms	**2.5**

* Number of rooms specifically designed for
sleeping quarters. Calculation of bedrooms for
certification purposes may be higher.

Efficient Living Rating

*Please note: Photographed home may have
been modified to suit homeowner's
preference.*

Detached garage plan available.

 Wall closets, if organized correctly, can provide comparable storage space to walk-in closets.

 Use an electric mulching mower to shred clippings and leave them on the lawn. This reduces consumption of fuel as well as provides the landscaping with a natural fertilzer.

 A detached garage, which is available separately on this plan, isolates chemicals and fumes away from the living space of the home.

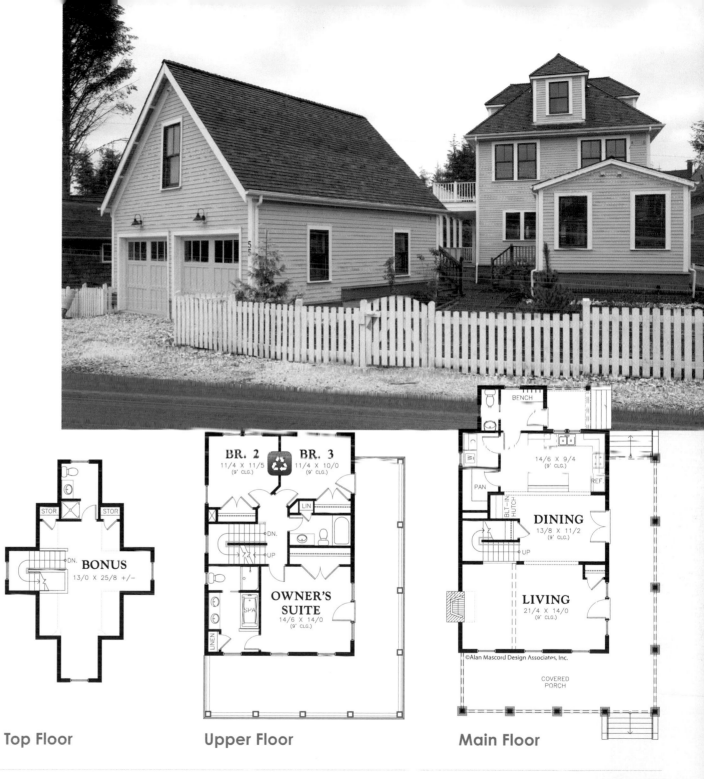

Top Floor

BONUS
13/0 X 25/8 +/-

Upper Floor

BR. 2
11/4 X 11/5
(9' CLG.)

BR. 3
11/4 X 10/0
(9' CLG.)

OWNER'S SUITE
14/6 X 14/0
(9' CLG.)

Main Floor

DINING
13/8 X 11/2
(9' CLG.)

LIVING
21/4 X 14/0
(9' CLG.)

14/6 X 9/4
(9' CLG.)

COVERED PORCH

©Alan Mascord Design Associates, Inc.

Materials & Resources

Sum of Many Parts

From its walls and windows to the furnishings and decorations you place within—your home is a sum of its many parts. The choices you make at each step—during construction and beyond—individually and collectively add to the end goal of producing a comfortable base for your life that is cost effective to operate, environmentally responsible, and a healthy place to live. There are many questions you might ask yourself when examining the choices ahead of you. Where do the components we use to build our homes come from? How long will they last? What are they made of? How do they perform? What are the alternatives? What will happen to them when we are finished? Do they give you satisfaction of ownership? Do they reflect your personality?

Determining the appropriateness and effectiveness of the components in our homes is of the utmost importance. As new technologies emerge, old technologies are reinvented, and styles change. Construction methods, recommendations and building codes change and adapt to improve the quality of our buildings and the health of our population. The development and adoption of testing and standards for materials and systems help builders and homeowners implement choices that have been examined to determine their practicality for use.

The suitability of one product or system over another depends on your deciding factors, and where they rank in importance to you. Look for standards that measure with your preferred ranking system, and then look for products that rate highly under that standard. Always consider the basic elements of health, practicality and sustainability when choosing components for your home: Will the product perform the task it's appointed for? Will the product deplete natural resources? Can the natural resources be replaced? Is it produced from chemicals that affect our environment? Can the product be returned to nature? Asking yourself these questions will ease the decision making process and lead to wise choices.

Life Cycle Assessment & Embodied Energy Costs

The total carbon footprint of your home is the sum of all of the energy and environmental costs of products you choose in its creation, and the materials and resources used during the life of the home. Life Cycle Assessment examines the individual components, and determines the energy and resource costs of manufacturing a product from the time raw materials are extracted to the time they are returned to nature or reused. Asking questions about the origin and destination of raw materials, the energy consumed in production and disposal, and of course the running costs of using the product helps us understand the embodied energy cost of a product. Performing a Life Cycle Assessment and considering the entire carbon footprint will determine the overall "greenness" of a material from a holistic approach and allow you to be certain it's as efficient and sustainable as you would expect.

Jobsite Recycling

When it comes to the jobsite, a smart way to be environmentally conscious is to order as many pre-fabricated items as possible. This will reduce the amount of waste you create on site. You might also decide to set up a job-site recycling center in order for your contractors to most easily separate plastics, paper, glass and wood. Investigate local companies that can recycle each of the items in your recycling center. Most importantly, be conscious of the materials you're throwing away. Double-check that purchase orders match your requirements before you buy something you don't need.

Be conscious of the materials you are throwing away. You may be able to use it for another purpose, removing it from the waste cycle altogether.

Local Products

Locally produced materials have less embodied energy costs—it requires less energy to transport them from their source and production location to your home site. Using local materials also supports the economy in the area in which you build. A product made from recycled content in China may not be as viable as one made from sustainable, virgin resources in your local area.

When making material choices for your home, consider the material's ability to withstand the elements to which it will be exposed. Naturally-occurring materials in any given location are most likely to be a good choice for homes in that area.

Environmentally Preferrable Products

Environmentally Preferable Products (EPPs) are products or services that have a lesser (or reduced) effect on human health and the environment, when compared to similar items created for the same purpose. Such products or services might incorporate recycled content, actively minimize waste, conserve energy/water, or reduce the amount of chemicals consumed and disposed.

Today, more and more products are made from recycled materials—from carpet and insulation to countertops and concrete. Buying building materials that contain recycled materials helps "close the recycling loop" by putting the materials we collect through recycling programs back to good use as products in the marketplace. To further innovation, look for products which have been created specifically to make use of materials previously destined for landfill.

There are many state, local, and nationally based programs and organizations in place to help consumers identify EPPs. Check your state and local government websites or go to the Environmental Protection Agency's website at www.epa.gov for more information.

Photo courtesy of Enviroglas

The Shell of Your Home

A well constructed shell (the exterior surfaces of your home-walls, siding, roof, etc.) is the primary step in creating an efficient home. The shell of your home protects you and all your belongings from the natural elements. The materials you choose to accomplish this task are the most important materials  you are likely to consider. Better construction means less possibility for weather intrusion and associated problems. Furthermore, a tight, well insulated, and sealed shell can significantly reduce the burden on the conditioning systems in your home, reducing your energy usage.

Beyond choosing the appropriate materials for a strong shell, consider how those materials will work with other systems employed in your home. For instance, when collecting rainwater from the roof to use on vegetables, an asphalt roof would not be compatible.

Design for Durability

Selecting materials for your home that will last throughout the building's entire lifespan will reduce maintenance and replacement cost; thereby reducing the lifecycle costs of the materials used. In addition, durable materials reduce the burden on natural resources, since they do not require frequent replacement. Building a durable home is an important aspect of being efficient. Elements that are exposed to weather and the Sun's rays should be a priority when selecting materials for durability. Your roof, siding and exterior elements need special attention.

A stained concrete floor, as shown above, is a durable flooring solution. See plan G21113 on page 66.

FSC Lumber

The majority of new homes are constructed from wood. From the roof trusses, to the wall studs and sheathing to floor systems, wood comprises a large part of the home's shell. In many forests around the world, logging to retrieve that wood still contributes to habitat destruction, water pollution, and violence toward or displacement of indigenous peoples and wildlife. Many consumers of wood and paper, and many forest products companies believe that the link between logging and these negative impacts can be broken, and that forests can be managed and protected at the same time. The Forest Stewardship Council (FSC) has developed and adopted practices and standards for friendly and sustainable logging practices. Wood harvested from forests by logging companies that have adopted these practices is referred to as FSC certified. Using FSC certified lumber in the construction of your home promotes environmental stewardship. Ask the manufacturers of your home products if the wood used in their products is certified and look for the FSC stamp of approval.

Insulation

Heating and cooling our living spaces accounts for 50 to 70% of the energy used in the average home. The over-conditioning of spaces due to inadequate insulation and air leakage are the leading causes of energy waste in most homes. High performing insulation in the walls, floors, and roof could be the best investment you put into your home. Remember that saving energy can help pay for original installation costs, meaning that the energy you conserve also translates to money saved: annual savings will only increase if utility rates continue to go up.

In addition to curbing energy waste, good insulation can also make your house more comfortable by helping to maintain a uniform temperature throughout the space and making it less "drafty". A home with well insulated walls, ceilings, and floors will feel warmer in the winter and cooler in the summer, reducing energy consumption year-round.

Types of insulation

As a general rule: the more insulation the better. Although this rule applies to all insulation types, they are not all created equal. While certain types are better in some applications than others, they all seek to accomplish the same thing: to create the best thermal break with highest R-value and least amount of air infiltration as possible in the given wall, floor, or roof cavity.

R-value is the number used to rate and measure a material's insulative properties. The higher the number, the better the insulative properties, and the more energy saved. When choosing an insulation, you should seek a product with the highest R-value for your budget and application.

Another important job of insulation is to aid in limiting the amount of air leakage between the interior and exterior of your home. The overall composition of the roof, floor, or wall system should minimize air leakage through all of it's components including caulking and sealing, the structural framing, exterior sheathing and siding, and interior surfaces. However, the insulation is your home's primary defense against leaking air. Some insulation types are better at sealing all the cavities than others.

Choosing the most effective insulation for your home may also require varying the types used in different cavity locations. Depending on your situation and budget, you may find that although spray foam insulation is better for a higher R-value per inch of thickness and is great for sealing cavities from air leakage in a narrow wall cavity, a blown-in insulation may be more cost effective in an attic space.

With all insulation types, in all applications, proper installation is key. Poor installation can dramatically reduce the material's insulating qualities, negating your investment in the material. Be sure to completely seal and insulate all surfaces in contact with the outside. Don't forget all wall cavities, floors under heated spaces, and especially roofs or attics. Some overlooked areas to note: the attic access door or hatch should be fully insulated. Concrete slabs under living spaces, and smaller cavities, such as in-framed wall corners and interior surfaces of window and door headers, should be considered.

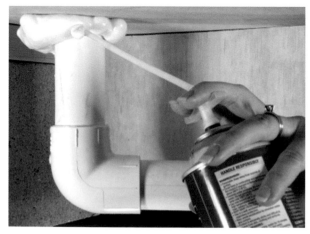

Seal all penetrations around ducts, pipes and electrical work with expanding foam to prevent air leakage.

Spray Foam

Made from natural plant oils, soy based spray foam offers the opportunity to insulate wall and roof spaces with a product that is both natural, environmentally responsible, and energy efficient. Non-plant based spray foams are also available; both are designed to expand and fill air cavities effectively. Spray foam comes in two varieties: Open cell is used in ventilated applications, closed cell may negate the need for providing ventilation space. Check manufacturer specifications and requirements.

Photo courtesy of Owens Corning, Inc.

Rigid

Made from fibrous materials or plastic foam (such as polyisocyanurate), rigid insulation is pressed into board-like forms and molded pipe-coverings. These provide thermal and acoustical insulation. Such boards may be faced with a reflective foil, which reduces heat flow when next to an air space. Rigid board can be applied to wall surfaces to provide a good thermal break between the interior and exterior air. With Structural Insulated Panels (SIPs) rigid insulation is sandwiched between wood panels to create an alternate wall system to using conventional studs and sheathing.

Blankets

Batts, or rolls, are flexible products made from mineral fibers or more environmentally preferable materials such as cotton from recycled denim jeans. They are available in widths suited to the standard spacing of wall studs and attic or floor joists. Continuous rolls can be hand-cut and trimmed to fit. They are also available with or without vapor retardant facings. Fiberglass batts are one of the most common of insulation types today because of their ease of installation and relative material cost. When thinking of using batts, consider using the more environmentally friendly material types such as cotton. Also note, that although basic installation of batts may be easy, it is essential that they are installed perfectly to perform at their highest rating.

Photo courtesy of Bonded Logic, Inc.

Blown-In

Loose-fill insulation includes loose fibers or fiber pellets that are blown into building cavities or attics using pneumatic equipment. Another form of blown-in insulation includes fibers that are co-sprayed with an adhesive to make them resistant to settling. The blown-in material can provide additional resistance to air infiltration if the insulation is sufficiently dense.

Thermal Bridges

The materials used to construct the shell of your home often have a poor insulating value, and require additional insulation. Where a framing member meets the sheathing material on the outside and the wallboard on the inside, there is no place to fit insulation, allowing cold or heat to "bridge" into your home this is called a thermal bridge. Different methods of construction can reduce the amount of thermal bridges in your building envelope: advanced framing, external insulating sheathing, and panel based systems such as Structural Insulated Panels (SIPs) are all employed to increase the thermal properties of your walls.

Shown below is an advanced framed technique known as a staggered stud wall. The staggered wall studs allow the insulation to "weave" between the studs and fill the corner cavities, eliminating the amount of thermal bridges. This wall system provides an overall deeper wall cavity (compared to a standard 2x6 stud wall framing system) to be filled with more insulation and raising the R-value of the wall system. This system proves to be a high performance alternative to standard stud framed walls.

Window Efficiency

Windows and glass doors can have a dramatic effect on the energy performance of a house. If not properly considered, they can be large thermal holes in your home. With today's ever advancing technology, windows and doors are achieving a wide variety of goals without compromising the amount of daylight emitted through the glazing, the visibility through the glazing, or the overall style or operability.

The NFRC label details the insulating and light transmittance levels of windows.

A wide variety of coatings, configurations, and frame materials are now available to achieve lower U-values and SHGC. A U-value is a measurable rating of energy performance, the rule of thumb is that the lower the U value, the better the performance. The SHGC or Solar Heat Gain Coefficient is the amount of radiated heat the glazing lets in. In most cases, the lower SHGC is more desirable for interior climate control. Although, with the correct passive solar design, you may want a higher SHGC on south facing glazing to take full advantage of the sun.

There are many options and types of windows for you to choose from. When picking your windows, be sure to consider not only the thermal performance of the window, but also the following:

• What type is appropriate for my home's architectural style? Some frame materials, profiles, and colors available may be more appropriate for your home's style than others.

• What type of maintenance is required to insure the windows will last the life of my home? Pay close attention to the durability of the windows. Be sure they are well built and can endure the weather

your home will experience. There are different cladding and frame material options including fiberglass, vinyl, wood, and aluminum. Some frame materials or exterior cladding surfaces will require less maintenance and are more resistant to the elements.

- Does the window type or manufacturer offer environmental friendly materials and practices in the construction of their windows? Will any of the materials used in the window will break down and release unhealthy toxins into the home? There are manufacturers who offer certified wood products in the construction of their windows.

Windows are a very important part of not only how your home performs thermally, but also of completing the architectural style. Consult with your design professional and window manufacturer or builder to be sure you are asking the right questions and choosing wisely.

Noise management

In addition to energy saving benefits, a well insulated home offers protection against environmental noise pollution. Sound travels in waves and flows, much like water or air. Any hole (or opening) that could let a draft in will likewise let noise in. Unwanted noise from planes, trains, traffic, loud car stereos and other nuisances can be eliminated by selecting appropriate wall systems and windows. A tight, well insulated, energy efficient building envelope greatly reduces the number of gaps in the wall system, offering extensive protection against sound intrusion. Installing high performance windows with insulated glass (possibly triple pane glass for ultimate noise reduction) will also reduce the amount of unwanted exterior noise.

Another way to understand and gauge noise management is with the Sound Transmission Class (STC) rating. The STC of a floor, wall or window assembly refers to how well such elements reduce sound or noise levels. The more noise a material dampens, the higher the rating. This rating directly reflects the number of decibels (dB) a material or assembly reduces. A standard interior wall assembly has an STC of about 35, meaning that a noise of 50dB (the level of a normal conversation) on the other side of the wall would sound like a noise of 15dB (the level of a very quiet whisper). For advanced noise and acoustic management in your home consult a professional.

For the best interior sound control, make sure to caulk and seal all joints and cracks in walls, ceilings and floors, and insulate all cavities between the rooms desired to be isolated. Additional measures include: installing a double layer of wall board (or sound reducing wall board), reducing the number of electrical and duct penetrations between rooms, and installing resilient channels between the wall board and studs to lessen vibrations. For even greater sound insulation, install a double row of staggered studs and fill both rows of framing with insulation.

Environmentally preferrable products include VOC free cabinetry, engineered quartz countertops, and recycled glass tile.

Finishes

The finishes of your home are where your personality and style are most on display. There are many options available for stylish and environmentally friendly interior and exterior finish materials. Rather than pointing you to many specific products, we offer a few suggestions for things to consider while seeking out that perfect finish material. Following these suggestions will ensure that your home is built and fashioned from materials that are in accordance with the sustainable measures you're achieving in the other aspects of your home construction.

First and foremost, does the material fit your style and the style of your home? With so many choices, there is no doubt an environmentally-friendly material that exists. Pick a finish that speaks to you and your home's unique architectural style and reflects your personality. Regarding the environmental friendliness of the finishes, the suggestions are similar to other discussions in this text. You should consider the material's complete life cycle and carbon footprint. Also, be sure to install finishes that are healthy and durable. Avoid products that contain materials such as vinyl that will outgas and put your indoor air quality at risk. Durable finishes will last longer and require less maintenance.

When considering floor materials, use inert materials wherever possible. This means your materials should be sustainable, VOC free, and non-porous. For example: stone, tile, sealed concrete, terra cotta, terrazzo, marmoleum, and ceramic tiles are some options. If carpet is a must, it's best to avoid glue-down carpet. Instead, look to low-VOC adhesives, carpet tiles, and carpets or area rugs that are pre-certified to meet green standards. Note that most carpets can pose health problems for chemically sensitive individuals due to the carpet material's strong absorption.

In addition to flooring, there are countless choices of responsible materials that can be used for wall treatments, countertops, millwork and cabinets. From dark granite-like surfaces made from recycled newsprint to slab surfaces made from recycled glass, you are bound to discover something that suits your preference. Paint and similar wall finishes are now available with reduced or no VOC to ensure healthy indoor air. Homebuilders and designers have countless options when it comes to choosing stylish, sustainable, and healthy finish materials.

Furnishings

There are so many environmentally responsible furniture choices available that no style or taste can go unsatisfied. Simply shop carefully. Consider the lifecycle costs and health implications of any furniture pieces you bring into your home. Determine if they have been made from responsible materials, and consider what will happen to them at the end of their use. As well as understanding the chemicals they may emit over their lifespan, consider how durable they are, or if they are easy to keep clean. For upholstered furniture pieces, try and select stylish materials that are tight woven, and do not collect dust that will detract from your air quality. For wood furniture, look for pieces that use certified wood products.

Alumont
Plan G21113

Sustainable Chic

At first glance, this home's geometric shapes, intersecting angles and palette of warm and bright colors draw your attention, but its creative touches don't end with the playful architecture: this unique home is loaded with eco-friendly features.

Embedded in the cheerful outer façade are a number of environmentally responsible and energy-efficient features; the first of which is related to the home's orientation. The house was designed to take advantage of the natural properties of the sun, with overhangs to block summer rays, windows positioned to allow heat and light to enter during cooler months, and interior materials selected to take advantage of that solar energy. The light colored metal roof is more durable than most alternatives and lasts longer, saving both building materials and money. It also allows the harvest of clean rainwater—for gardening or watering—that has not been contaminated with the chemical runoff from traditional roofing materials.

The exterior also employs fiber cement siding, composed of recycled materials.

The exquisite landscaping features a xeriscaped area; large flags of stone with spaces in-between that are filled with rocks, allowing water to percolate naturally into the ground while being easy to maintain and have no watering requirement. Separate beds for trees and greenery are interspersed, minimizing yard upkeep, weeding and water consumption.

Inside, the benefits of the home's water heating system is twofold: radiant heated floors and no need for a central water storage tank. The hot water piping system embedded in the concrete flooring circulates heat directly to people, objects and furnishings. The flooring is stained concrete, which is sealed with a colored finish and varnish to make it non-porous. (See photo on page 61.) The sealed concrete floor looks attractive and stays comfortably warm without the use and extra expense of additional flooring materials. The

Photography ©Bob Greenspan

This kitchen takes advantage of using sustainable materials, such as quartz countertops and FSC-certified wood cabinets.

walls are covered with no-VOC paint, which does not emit the dangerous chemicals of regular paint, making the air inside the home safer to breathe.

The kitchen countertops are engineered quartz, a material made of rock dust that is impervious to bacteria, unlike other popular granite surfaces. It is also more environmentally friendly, reducing the use of natural resources of stone slab material. In the main bathroom, a mixture of recycled glass and concrete forms the countertop. The hardwood stairs leading to the second floor are a farmed hardwood, maximizing style and durability while remaining conscious of the use of natural materials.

Throughout this home, the owner has made product choices that reflect Efficient Living values, from low-voltage light bulbs and low-flow showerheads to white, natural curtains for reflecting light during the day and trapping heat inside at night. Another original choice for this home was the all-natural carpeting, made of wool (no gasses or dyes involved in production) with a hemp fiber backing. The owner also selected high-efficiency ENERGY STAR appliances, which not only reduce energy bills and preserve resources, but are also eligible for government rebates. All in all, this home stands out as a model of originality, from its outer aesthetic to its environmentally conscientious details.

Home Facts

Alumont

Plan G21113 Price Code **C**

Living Space	Sq Ft
Upper Floor	721
Main Floor	1178
Total Living Space	**1,899**

Width	40'-0"
Depth	57'-0"
Bedrooms	2*
Bathrooms	2.5

* Number of rooms specifically designed for sleeping quarters. Calculation of bedrooms for certification purposes may be higher.

Efficient Living Rating

 Instead of carpeting, consider a stained concrete floor or hardwood. It's low maintenance and beneficial for indoor air quality.

Windows on adjacent sides of a room offer balanced light throughout, thus reducing the need for artificial light sources.

Simple shed roofs on this plan are an efficient framing approach and cost effective feature.

Operable windows close to the ceiling allow rising warm air to escape in the summer months, and provide daylight to the entry below.

i This plan offers a sauna. If you prefer, use this space as additional storage.

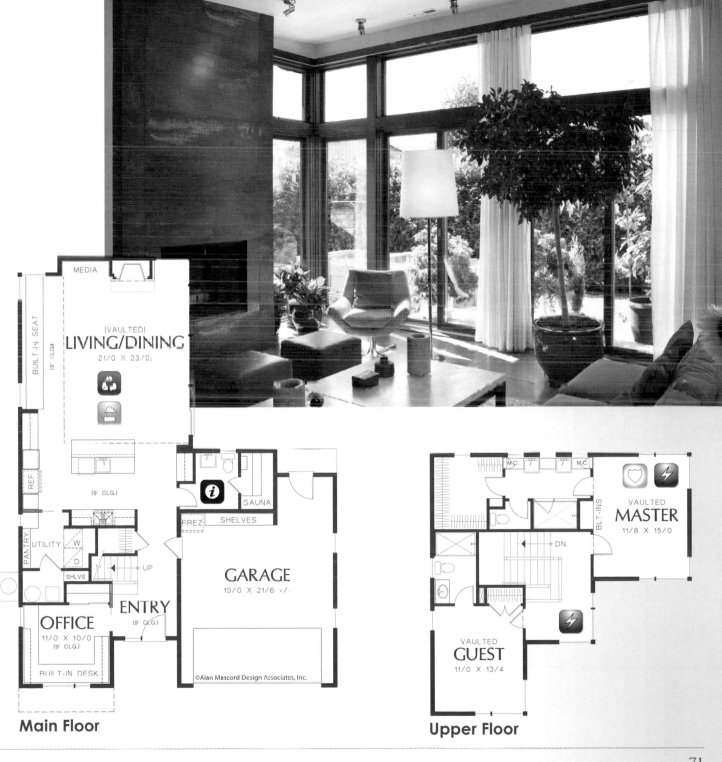

MEDIA

BUILT-IN SEAT

(VAULTED)
LIVING/DINING
21/0 X 23/0
(9' CLG.)

(9' CLG.)

REF

PANTRY

UTILITY

W
D

SHLVS

UP

OFFICE
11/0 X 10/0
(9' CLG.)

BUILT-IN DESK

ENTRY
(9' CLG.)

SAUNA

FREZ

SHELVES

GARAGE
19/0 X 21/6 +/-

©Alan Mascord Design Associates, Inc.

Main Floor

M.C.   M.C.

VAULTED
MASTER
11/8 X 15/0

BLT-INS

DN.

VAULTED
GUEST
11/0 X 13/4

Upper Floor

71

Upper Floor

©Alan Mascord Design Associates, Inc.

Main Floor

©Alan Mascord Design Associates, Inc.

Home Facts

Skycole

Plan G21107 Price Code **B**

Living Space	Sq Ft
Upper Floor	769
Main Floor	434
Total Living Space	**1,203**

Width	17'-0"
Depth	58'-0"
Bedrooms	2*
Bathrooms	2

* Number of rooms specifically designed for sleeping quarters. Calculation of bedrooms for certification purposes may be higher.

Efficient Living Rating

Centralized plumbing fixtures reduce installation material costs and offer energy savings throughout the life span of the home.

House plans with a compact footprint reduce floor framing labor and materials.

Eliminating the laundry room and installing a washer/dryer in a closet can save floor area on smaller plans.

Home Facts

Creswell

Plan G2175 Price Code **B**

Living Space	Sq Ft
Upper Floor	809
Main Floor	655
Total Living Space	**1,464**

Width	30'-0"
Depth	42'-0"
Bedrooms	3*
Bathrooms	2.5

* Number of rooms specifically designed for sleeping quarters. Calculation of bedrooms for certification purposes may be higher.

Efficient Living Rating

 See the DVD to view this kitchen in 3D, explore appliance options and to learn more about efficient living.

 Avoid driving at peak rush hour times so that your car does not idle for long periods of time. This will improve air quality as well as cut down on fuel waste. Avoiding stop and go driving will also reduce wear and tear on your car.

 Large, south-facing roof planes provide ample space for incorporating photovoltaic panels.

Window shades can be used to reduce heat let in from the sun, thus reducing the need for air conditioning.

Upper Floor

BR. 3
10/0 X 10/0

MASTER
12/0 X 13/0

LINEN

DN

FOYER BELOW

BR. 2
11/0 X 11/8

©Alan Mascord Design Associates, Inc.

DINING
10/0 X 10/0

GREAT RM.
15/0 X 13/0
(9' CLG.)

RANGE

REF

P

STOR.

UP

GARAGE
19/0 X 19/6 +

©Alan Mascord Design Associates, Inc.

Main Floor

BONUS
13/0 X 13/9

LOFT
13/0 X 12/4

ⓘ

Top Floor

BR. 2
11/4 X 11/6
(9' CLG.)

BR. 3
11/4 X 10/0
(9' CLG.)

LIN

DN.

UP

SPA

LINEN

MASTER
14/6 X 14/0
(9' CLG.)

DECK

Upper Floor

Home Facts
Eaton
Plan G22171A Price Code **D**

Living Space	Sq Ft
Loft	542
Upper Floor	801
Main Floor	941
Total Living Space	**2,284**
Width	**24'-0"**
Depth	**43'-0"**
Bedrooms	**3***
Bathrooms	**3.5**

* Number of rooms specifically designed for sleeping quarters. Calculation of bedrooms for certification purposes may be higher.

Efficient Living Rating

Detached garage plan available.

BENCH

W. D.

PAN

14/6 X 9/4
(9' CLG.)

REF

BLT-IN HUTCH

DINING
13/2 X 11/4
(9' CLG.)

UP

STORAGE

WINDOW SEAT

STORAGE

LIVING
21/4 X 14/0
(9' CLG.)

©Alan Mascord Design Associates, Inc.

Main Floor

ⓘ Keep hazardous waste out of the trash. It can leak into the water supply and pollute the air. Take any hazardous chemicals to the landfill or recycling center so they can be disposed of properly.

Choose cleaning materials that contain natural ingredients.

ⓘ This plan takes advantage of the volume under the roof for a flexible loft and bonus space.

Consider air drying clothes on a clothes line or drying rack to reduce energy consumption. Also consider washing all of your clothes in cold water. The strength of today's laundry detergents eliminates the need to use hot water. This requires less energy to heat the water, and will lengthen the life of your clothes.

Home Facts

Ellwood

Plan G21103 Price Code **C**

Living Space	Sq Ft
Upper Floor	430
Main Floor	1514
Total Living Space	**1,944**

Width	45'-0"
Depth	55'-0"
Bedrooms	3*
Bathrooms	2.5

* Number of rooms specifically designed for sleeping quarters. Calculation of bedrooms for certification purposes may be higher.

Efficient Living Rating

Wash and dry full loads. If you are washing a small load, use the appropriate water setting.

Consider a shower instead of a bath. The amount of water needed to fill a tub varies, but on average, a bath uses 15 to 25 gallons of hot water, compared to less than 10 gallons for a shower.

Turn off your computer and monitor when not in use. When idle screen savers use just as much energy.

Main Floor

Upper Floor

Home Facts

Huntington
Plan G4027C Price Code **G**

Living Space	Sq Ft
Upper Floor	661
Main Floor	695
Total Living Space	**1,356**

Width	42'-0"
Depth	41'-0"
Bedrooms	3*
Bathrooms	2.5

* Number of rooms specifically designed for sleeping quarters. Calculation of bedrooms for certification purposes may be higher.

Efficient Living Rating

To ensure your heating and cooling systems are operating efficiently, make sure all ductwork in the house is sealed completely and properly.

Clustered housing developments offer many environmental benefits. More densely sited homes use less land, allowing the remaining land for wildlife habitat and natural areas.

Area information is per unit.

Detached garage plan available.

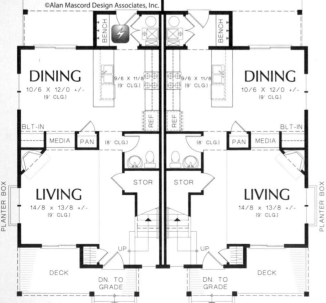

©Alan Mascord Design Associates, Inc.

DINING
10/6 X 12/0 +/-
(9' CLG.)

9/6 X 11/8 (9' CLG.)

9/6 X 11/8 (9' CLG.)

DINING
10/6 X 12/0 +/-
(9' CLG.)

BENCH

BENCH

REF

REF

BLT-IN

MEDIA PAN

PAN MEDIA

BLT-IN

(8' CLG.)

(8' CLG.)

LIVING
14/8 x 13/8 +/-
(9' CLG.)

STOR

STOR

LIVING
14/8 x 13/8 +/-
(9' CLG.)

PLANTER BOX

PLANTER BOX

UP

UP

DECK

DN. TO GRADE

DN. TO GRADE

DECK

Main Floor

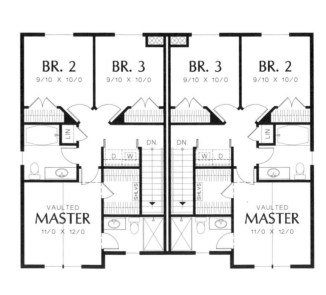

BR. 2
9/10 X 10/0

BR. 3
9/10 X 10/0

BR. 3
9/10 X 10/0

BR. 2
9/10 X 10/0

LIN

LIN

D W

DN.

DN.

W D

SHLVS

SHLVS

VAULTED
MASTER
11/0 X 12/0

VAULTED
MASTER
11/0 X 12/0

Upper Floor

Home Facts

Prairiefire
Plan G4041 Price Code **G**

Living Space	Sq Ft
Upper Floor	1.212
Main Floor	1,158
Lower Floor	491
Total Living Space	**2,861**
Width	60'-0"
Depth	52'-0"
Bedrooms	3*
Bathrooms	2.5

* Number of rooms specifically designed for sleeping quarters. Calculation of bedrooms for certification purposes may be higher.

Efficient Living Rating

Area information is per unit.
Plan designed for up-sloping lot

 A shared wall can reduce energy costs for each unit. Only 3 walls are exposed to the elements.

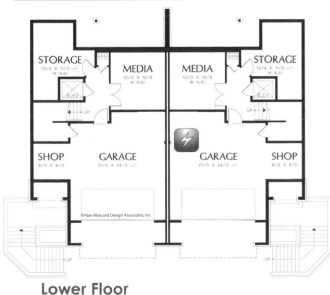

Lower Floor

Main Floor

Upper Floor

Energy

⚡ Energy

How much does energy cost? The exact price of energy extends well beyond the numbers on a utility bill. Different sources of energy have different associated costs, and, furthermore, the elements we choose to use in our homes increase or decrease the amount of energy we consume.

Understanding what energy costs are and where they come from empowers us; once equipped with such knowledge, we become inspired to make smart choices to reduce our energy overhead and utility bills. What's more, this can be done without altering our lifestyles and chosen comforts.

As discussed extensively, one of the core principles of efficient living is understanding how our own unique ways of life (our homes and their possessions) impact our living environments. This principle is befitting when we talk about energy efficiency. Energy is used to heat, cool, light our homes, to cook our food, power our cars and provide us with entertainment, and the cost of doing all these activities is on the rise.

Energy efficiency is one of the most illustrative areas in the current environmental conditions by which a few very small steps, taken by many people, can result in a very large change of course. The smallest change or purchase decision can have a very measurable impact in our homes, which extends into our environment, and ultimately to the planet. Consider this: if every American home replaced just one incandescent light bulb with an ENERGY STAR-qualified bulb, it would save enough energy to light more than 3 million homes for a year. It would also save more than 600 million dollars in annual energy costs and it would prevent greenhouse gases equivalent to the emissions of more than 800,000 cars.

As an added bonus to forging a significant impact on our collective environment, we'll find smaller impacts on our individual pocket books. Taking small steps toward curbing energy use is undeniably win-win.

Your Home—The Machine

The systems in your home are invariably connected. They interact with one another in ways you might not consciously be aware of. For instance, improving the level of insulation in your home can decrease the size of heating equipment required. This could result in serious savings (and that's before even looking at the energy efficiency of the heating equipment itself). Some choices you make may even negate the requirement of other systems altogether, such as matching radiant floor heating with an integrated water heating system where there is no requirement for a separate furnace and duct system.

Passive and Active Conditioning

Some of the systems used to heat and cool your home run automatically, and some require your intervention. Passive systems, such as operable windows used for cross ventilation, offer low running costs because of the lack of automation. Think of it in these terms—passive systems are for active people. Because of the lack of automation, passive systems often need more intervention than a mechanical system. For example, manual window shades (passive) work ONLY if they are drawn, yet the shades also need to be opened when heat and light are needed.

Consider what work you are willing to put into a system before you commit to it. In the event that you underestimate the amount of work involved, you may end up supplementing the system with another, or at least spending much more time and energy than you might have anticipated.

Mechanical systems, on the other hand, offer automation and perhaps less maintenance; but they usually have a higher energy cost associated. Below you'll find information, tips and helpful hints for both passive and active systems in your home.

Passive Conditioning Systems

Passive systems utilize the scientific properties of natural elements. For example, different materials warm and cool at different rates, heat moves from warm to cold, and warm air rises. Understanding how nature works enable us to design systems that use those properties to our advantage, without the need for power consuming mechanical equipment. Below are a couple of elements you may find in a passive conditioning system.

Cross Ventilation

Adequate ventilation in an efficient home is extremely important. Cross ventilation uses the scientific properties of air to provide fresh air indoors. To achieve cross ventilation, especially during summer, open windows on each side of the house at night. Because the outdoor air is cooler, warm, stale air indoors is vented to the outside, since heat moves from warm to cold. This provides fresh air for occupants as well as reducing the need for cooling. Don't forget to close windows during the day to prevent warmer outdoor air from entering your cooler home.

Passive Solar Design and Thermal Mass

The natural properties of dense materials such as concrete and stone mean they can hold and release heat slowly. We can harness these properties by using the sun to heat those elements, and let them release the heat slowly after sunset. During the heating season, it's most effective to leave shades and blinds open on sunny days, and then close them at night to reduce the amount of heat lost through the windows. Close shades and blinds during the summer or when the air conditioner is in use to prevent sunlight from heating the thermal mass element.

Ceiling Fans

Ceiling fans are used to control the comfort level in homes. Contrary to popular belief, ceiling fans don't actually cool the air in your house, but they make you feel cooler by providing a breeze. Having a breeze may allow you to raise the temperature in the room while remaining comfortable, which reduces the amount of cooling you need to remain comfortable. Fans, therefore, are used to supplement passive cooling systems and reduce the necessity for air conditioning units. ENERGY STAR rated fans are available on most models.

Mechanical Conditioning Systems

Mechanical systems can use a variety of elements to heat and cool your home, thereby conditioning it. These elements might include hydronic systems (which use water to transfer heat), systems that heat air and move it to the required location, or electrical systems which control temperature using fans and heating elements. No matter which you choose for your home there are ways to increase your conditioning system's efficiency.

Zoned Heating

Zoned heating systems use thermostats in each room or multiple 'zones' to control the flow of air or hot water around a central heating system, directing energy to the place in the home where it is needed most. By individually controlling the temperature in each zone, you will reduce the overall load on the heat source—therefore lowering the amount of energy consumed.

In a ducted system, dampers or bladders in the ductwork block the flow of warm air to rooms that are already at the desired temperature set on the thermostat. In a hydronic system, valves control the flow of water in the same manner.

Efficient Furnaces

If you are using a forced air system, the key to saving energy is correctly sizing the equipment. After calculating the heating requirements considering the size of your house and efficiency of your wall and window systems using *ACCA Manual J* (www.acca.org), the heat source and ductwork needs to be correctly sized to efficiently distribute the conditioned air using *ACCA Manual D*. Heat loss and equipment sizing calculations should be performed by a professional HVAC contractor.

The efficiency of new furnaces is measured by the Annual Fuel Utilization Efficiency (AFUE) rating, a measure of seasonal performance. Today, standard furnaces are between 78% AFUE and 96% AFUE. The higher the AFUE percentage, the more efficient the furnace unit. Consult the Energy Label when selecting the furnace. Although there are options for both gas and electric furnaces, a gas furnace may be more attractive from a utility cost perspective. However, a gas furnace can also use a significant amount of electricity, mostly to power the fan motor. Variable speed fan motors are generally more efficient than standard motors and may save you hundreds of dollars per year.

The distribution of conditioned air is as important as the heat source. The things to consider when sizing ductwork are the length of the duct run, the size of the tubing, and volume of space being conditioned. Ductwork should be properly sealed to prevent distribution loss.

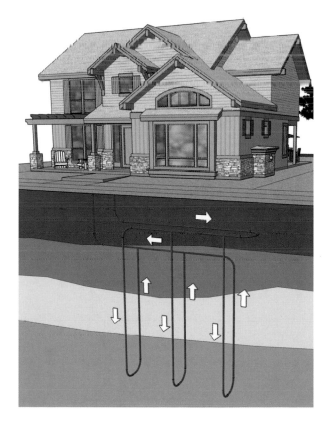

Heat Pumps

With a ducted system, a heat pump offers an alternative to a furnace. A heat pump is an air conditioner that moves heat from one place to another using a heat transfer fluid; heating or cooling your spaces. Even during colder months, heat from outdoor air can be extracted and transferred to the interior of your home. During summer, the heat pump removes heat from the air inside your home and transfers it to the outside. Heat pumps offer substantial energy savings over gas furnaces with reduced annual operating costs of up to 40% .

One way to further reduce the amount of energy needed to cool your home with a heat pump is to install a mister on the outdoor unit. Water on the unit evaporates making it more efficient at releasing heat outdoors.

Contrasting a typical air source heat pump which uses outside air to condition the heat transfer fluid, geo-exchange systems use the constant temperature of the earth to heat and cool your home. What does that mean? Essentially, a heat transfer fluid used in the conditioning unit is pumped through a loop running into the ground or beneath a body of water before being transferred back to the unit. Because the earth is a constant temperature, cooler fluid is warmed, and warmer fluid is cooled. The conditioner then uses a compressor to adjust the temperature of the pre-conditioned fluid to the desired level for use in your home. The length of the loop required varies depending on loop placement, ground temperature, thermal conductivity of the ground, soil moisture, and system design. Pipes can be laid horizontally, vertically, or at the bottom of a pond. These closed loop systems have become the most common of geo-exchange systems.

In a Geo-Exchange system, tubing is installed to take advantage of the constant ground temperature of the planet.

Radiant Heating

Radiant systems differ from forced air systems in the way they warm you and your surroundings. Rather than heating air, these systems depend largely on radiant heat transfer—which is the delivery of heat directly from a surface itself to the people and objects in the room. In hydronic systems water is heated and delivered to radiators on or near the wall or in floor tubing. In the case of in floor heating, heat is transferred from the tubing directly to the floor surface and objects in the room, using them to evenly heat the spaces they occupy. Tubing can be laid in numerous ways. It can be placed in between the floor joists with a heat reflector plate, on top of floor joists in a 'subfloor sandwich', in a thin concrete topping, or in a concrete slab floor. Consult a professional for assistance in choosing the most appropriate in-floor system for your circumstances. Since radiant heat warms people and objects directly, occupants are often more comfortable at a lower temperature setting than might be used with a traditional, forced air heating system. In addition, heat distributed evenly reduces cold spots in your room.

To supply radiant floor heating to small spaces such as tile floors in bathrooms; smaller electric systems may be appropriate. When installing a radiant floor system consider the finished flooring material's dimensional stability and heat conductive properties.

Hydronic in-floor radiant tubes. Image courtesy of Warm Floors, Inc.

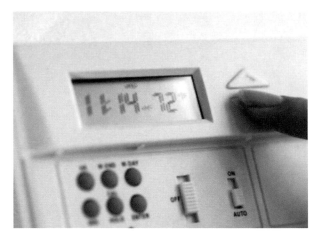

Taking Control of Temperature

Being comfortable in your home carries the utmost importance. At the correct humidity level, most people feel comfortable at 68 degrees. With that in mind, there are flexible ways of approaching temperature that can save energy and reduce your electric bill. Temperature is obviously adjustable, but how often do you adjust the temperature of your home for when you're out of the house or asleep? In the wintertime, it's best to set your thermostat to the low 60's while you're away during the daytime, and 55 degrees before going to sleep at night. A programmable thermostat can be used to automate the temperature selection process.

We can also use temperature settings to reduce the amount of energy we consume when heating water. One way is to set the thermostat on your water heater between 100 and 120 degrees. Hotter water often needs cooling with cold water at the point of use to be comfortable to the touch, thus negating the reason for heating it above 120 degrees.. It's possible to lower the temperature even further for bathing and washing, but below 100 degrees you may run out of stored hot water. Before making adjustments to your water temperature, check the required temperature of water for your dishwasher, since some models require higher temperatures. Besides adjusting the temperature setting, there are also other elements to help you increase the efficiency of your water heating system.

Water Heating Systems

With a storage tank system, use a high efficiency ENERGY STAR rated model. Wrap your water heater in an insulating jacket. This measure alone can save 1,100 lbs. of CO_2 per year for an electric water heater, or 220 lbs for a gas heater. Along with using an efficient water heater, the water distribution system should be carefully isulated to prevent heat loss between the source (your heater) and destination (appliance or faucet). Consider installing plumbing chases below floor joists to minimize plumbing runs; the less water has to travel from the heat source to the destination, the less time it has to cool. Insulate all hot water distribution pipes to R4 or above to minimize losses.

An alternative to a storage tank water heater is an on-demand (or instant) water heater. These water heaters do not store heated water constantly, but rather heat the water when it's needed. On demand water heaters, therefore, reduce the amount of energy consumed preemptively heating water; they are also much smaller and require less mechanical space than storage tank systems.

Shown above is a combined space and water heating system with radiant floor heating manifold. Image courtesy of Warm Floors, Inc.

Electrical Systems

A large part of the energy we consume is through our use of technology beyond the light switches and entertainment systems in our homes. As more electronic devices become a regular part of our lifestyles, we can analyze our use of those devices and utilize that information to reduce the amount of energy they consume.

Residual Power Consumption

The electronic items we operate in our home use power even when we're not using them—while they are in stand-by mode. While certainly a convenient feature for the consumer, the stand-by mode means these electronics literally consume power while waiting to be used. A simple step to curb this is to plug all your electronics into a power-strip. Power strips can then easily be switched off when you're not using them. If turning a power strip on and off frequently seems like a hassle, automatic power-strips are available which can automate the actions. One recent innovation in this area of residual power consumption includes the development of whole house switches, which can be used to turn off all selected electrical devices in the home with a single flip of a switch.

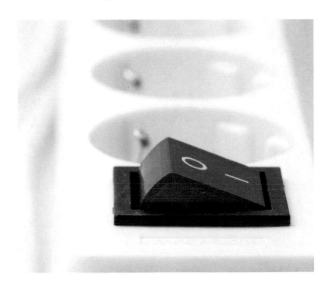

Computers & Technology

There are settings on your computer system designed to reduce the amount of energy the system consumes. Don't forget to enable the "sleep mode" feature on your computer which allows it to use less power during periods of inactivity. On most personal computers the power management settings are found on your control panel. Mac users, look for energy saving settings under system preferences in the "Apple" menu. Another way to make your computer more efficient is to configure your computer so that it will 'hibernate' automatically after 30 minutes or so of inactivity. This 'hibernate mode' turns the computer off in such a way that you won't be required to reload everything when you switch it back on. Computers can also help you reduce your energy consumption further; analytic software attached to sensors in equipment can detail your energy efficiency on the fly. Future developments in this area promise instant feedback on home energy consumption.

Using Lights Appropriately

It may sound obvious, but often we forget—turning out the light when you leave a room reduces energy consumption. In addition, installing dimmer switches on appropriate lighting fixtures allows you to adjust the light level to the task at hand and time of day (this is particularly appropriate at dusk, when natural light is available and only requires a little indoor help). Innovation in the area of motion and light sensing technology has given rise to the development of tools to help us automate such tasks. Bathrooms and closets are places where a motion sensing switch might help reduce the time the light (or fan) is left on. Be aware, however, that the motion sensor will use power to operate—therefore it's advisable to only install these types of switches in places where leaving the light on for long periods of time happens very frequently. When motion sensors are able to correct such behavior, the homeowner can experience significant savings.

Light fixtures with regular incandescent light bulbs installed use a significant amount of energy. ENERGY STAR light fixtures are available, and there are also alternatives for the bulbs you use in any fixture.

Compact Fluorescent Lights (CFLs)

ENERGY STAR qualified CFLs provide great savings in fixtures that are on for a substantial amount of time each day. At a minimum, ENERGY STAR recommends installing qualified CFLs in fixtures that are used at least 15 minutes at a time or several hours per day. In order to identify the best fixtures to use qualified CFLs, look to the rooms with the most use and traffic, such as family and living rooms, kitchens, dining rooms, bedrooms, and outdoor areas.

ENERGY STAR Qualified CFL Facts:

- CFLs use about 75% less energy than standard incandescent bulbs and last up to 10 times longer. (Which often translates to years longer).

- CFLs save about $30 or more in electricity costs over each bulb's lifetime.

- CFLs produce about 75% less heat—in addition to being safer to operate, they also cut energy costs associated with home cooling.

- For your own individual tastes and needs, CFLs are available in different sizes and shapes to fit in almost any fixture, for indoors and outdoors, including dimmable light fixtures.

Information about CFLs provided by ENERGY STAR. For more information visit *www.energystar.gov*

LED Lights

What is an LED? A Light Emitting Diode (LED) is a semiconductor device that converts electricity into light. Though the concept of LED lighting is over 40 years old, recent innovation in the technology has allowed LED lights to make their way into residential homes. Since LED lights convert most of their energy to light instead of heat they are cool to the touch, which can actually reduce the cooling your home requires during summer.

LED lights are more damage resistant than traditional incandescent bulbs and even CFLs. Note that using a 10-watt LED light instead of a 100-watt incandescent light would reduce your CO_2 emissions by more than 9,000 lbs over the life of the bulb.

75 feet of skylights were positioned to provide an abundance of natural light throughout plan 1412. To see more of this home, visit www.mascordefficientliving.com

Thoughtful Daylighting Strategies

Energy efficient lighting is about much more than the ratings or usage of an individual light bulb. While finding the most light for the least wattage is vital, addressing the quality of interior spaces by harnessing natural light to its fullest potential helps us achieve a higher level of efficiency.

Window Placement

Windows are an incredibly important element in an energy-efficient home. The correct placement of windows in relation to the sun is the first step to reducing your need for artificial lighting. To further improve quality, correctly placed windows will balance the interior light. Windows along a single wall at the end of a long room can create a tunnel effect. Adding windows on adjacent walls allows light to reflect on all sides of the room, making it appear much more spacious and improving the quality of the natural daylight.

Using Color

In addition to having a well-designed floor plan that harnesses the available natural light, light-colored interiors can reduce the need for artificial lighting by utilizing the natural properties of color. Simply painting your room in light colors can save energy. Light colored window shades can reflect unwanted rays from the sun—which protects your home from overheating and provides a method of adjusting the light level indoors.

Skylights and Solar Tubes

Well placed skylights can provide natural daylighting in areas which would otherwise be dark. Corridors, bathrooms and interior utility rooms can be transformed into bright, warm areas without the use of additional power. Solar tubes can be placed where skylights aren't possible. With their use of internal reflective material, solar tubes are very effective at harnessing the same bright daylight as a traditional skylight within more challenging spaces.

Natural Lighting

Window space is maximized on the south side of this home. Suitable overhangs protect the home from unwanted summer rays, yet allow the home to harness the properties of the Sun in wintertime. Light colored walls add a feeling of warmth while utilizing the full potential of the natural light available.

Appliances

Along with choosing an efficient appliance package, the way you actually use your appliances will have a strong effect on your energy consumption. Here are a few tips to help you reduce your energy use:

Washing Machines

When washing clothes, it's always vital to set the appropriate water level for the size of the load. Remember to wash in cold water when practical and always rinse in cold. When you need to wash your articles in hot water, consider reducing to warm water. Switching from hot to warm water for two loads per week can save nearly 500 lbs. of CO_2 per year if you have an electric water heater, or 150 lbs. for a gas heater.

Dryers

Remember to clean the dryer's lint filter after each use. Dry heavy and light fabrics separately and don't add wet items to a load that's already partially dry. If available, use your dryer's moisture sensor setting. Of course, limiting dryer use is the most sustainable choice—a clothesline is the most energy-efficient clothes dryer of all!

Left: Photo courtesy of Whirlpool® Home Appliances

Ovens

The most useful tip to save energy with your oven is to only open the oven door when needed. It may seem intuitive, but it really does help. Check the seal on the oven door, and use a microwave oven for cooking or reheating small items.

Refrigerators

Set your refrigerator temperature at 38 to 42 degrees Fahrenheit; your freezer should be set between 0 and 5 degrees Fahrenheit. Check to see if your refrigerator has a power save switch, and use it if it does. Make sure the door on your refrigerator seals tightly. You can check this by closing a dollar bill in between the door gaskets: if it's not difficult to pull out, or if it slides easily between the gaskets, replace them. Losing dollars here means you lose money constantly!

Dishwashers

Only turn your dishwasher on when you have a full load. Use short cycles for all but the dirtiest of dishes. In addition to saving water, this also saves you the costs associated with the energy used to heat it. Air-drying, if you have the time, can also reduce energy use. Dishwashers have the ability to turn off the drying cycle manually. Choosing not to use heat in the drying cycle can save 20% or more of your dishwasher's total energy use. Although it seems like it might be more water-conscious to wash dishes by hand, using an ENERGY STAR rated dishwasher wisely actually uses less water!

ENERGY STAR *rated appliances like the
refrigerator and dishwasher above are available
in attractive new finishes like Oiled Bronze
from Jenn-Air Home Appliances.*

87

Free Power

After taking steps to reduce your power consumption (and installing efficient systems to heat and cool your home) you might even want to consider harnessing natural energy and using it to generate your own power on site. Self-generation can lower or even zero out your energy bills. Homes that produce enough of their own energy to cover their consumption for the entire year are termed 'Net Zero' (self generated energy that is sold to utility companies at peak production times is bought back at peak consumption times, leaving a zero balance). Producing more power than you consume can even provide these homes (meaning you!) with a positive balance.

Water Heating

There are ways we can harness natural energy to heat (or, in some cases, cool) the water we use indoors. Depending on your geographical location, the options available to you may vary. Geo-thermal water heaters use the constant temperature of the earth to pre-heat the water, while Solar thermal water heating systems harness the power of the sun to provide hot water for indoor use, space heating, and pool heaters. In a geo-thermal system, water is run through a loop buried in the ground and is warmed by the earth. With a solar hot water heater, water is run through thin pipes across a surface that has been subjected to solar radiation. The water is then collected in a tank and used with appropriate supplemental heating equipment. In both solar and geo-thermal systems the water is already warm when it enters the water heater, and requires less energy to get it to the desired temperature for use.

Above: *Using United Solar Ovonic's UNI-SOLAR® shingles, Oakland University in Rochester, MI, has taken the lead in real-world alternative energy systems with the installation of a thin-film solar roof on a student community center.*

Left: *Even if Photo-voltaics are out of your current budget, pre-wiring for solar allows you to easily take advantage of the technology at a later date.*

Photo-Voltaic Power Systems

Photo-voltaic systems, while varied, usually involve arrays and shingles. Arrays can be installed on roof planes or in panel banks as part of landscaping. Solar shingles can be incorporated into the roofing material as shown below, or panels can be used as sunshades.

Solar arrays come in all sorts of shapes and sizes. Innovation in solar technology and production continues to expand the choices available, maintaining a consistent sense of architectural style while providing a means of harnessing the sun's energy.

Harnessing Wind

Wind has been a source of energy for many generations. Windmills use kinetic energy to harness wind and drive mechanical systems. In addition, wind turbines are used to convert air movement into electricity. A wind turbine like the one shown below can supplement a solar system during overcast winter days, and offer a space efficient method of power generation to homes unable to take advantage of solar power.

Jamieson
Plan G2178

Living Large on a Small Footprint

This contemporary-styled home takes "environmentally conscious" to a chic new level. Its appearance is inviting, but looks are where the similarity ends. Rather than wood, this home is encased in fiber cement siding, which does nature a favor by putting recycled material to good use while protecting the environment. Before construction began; thoughtful consideration to take advantage of natural light played a large factor in the home's orientation and finished design. As a result, the windows were situated to utilize the sun's warmth in winter and to avoid direct sunlight in the summer.

Inside, the home manages to feel spacious despite its narrow footprint, thanks to a well-designed interior and open floor plan. Adding to that spacious element is built-in furniture, conveniently tucked into alcoves in the walls and maximizing space in the kitchen and dining rooms. For the owner, the built-in shelves and seating are not only convenient and attractive; they also cut down on extra furnishing costs. In the colorful kitchen, the choice was made to build a 12" deep pantry, cutting out the wasted space of typical walk-in pantries and preserving essential storage space in an efficient, compact area.

The home owners chose to get creative and finish the floor with stained and sealed waferboard, bypassing the usual choice of finishing materials such as hardwood or tile. This choice was not only cost effective, allowing the homeowners to disperse funds to other areas of the home, but a conscience choice to prevent dust build-up.

To the smallest detail, this quaint home makes the most of an efficient floor plan and narrow lot to benefit both its owners and the environment.

Photography ©Bob Greenspan

Home Facts

Jamieson

Plan G2178 Price Code **B**

Living Space	Sq Ft
Upper Floor	863
Main Floor	558
Total Living Space	**1,421**
Width	**22'-0"**
Depth	**46'-0"**
Bedrooms	**3***
Bathrooms	**2**

* Number of rooms specifically designed for sleeping quarters. Calculation of bedrooms for certification purposes may be higher.

Efficient Living Rating

Upper Floor

Main Floor

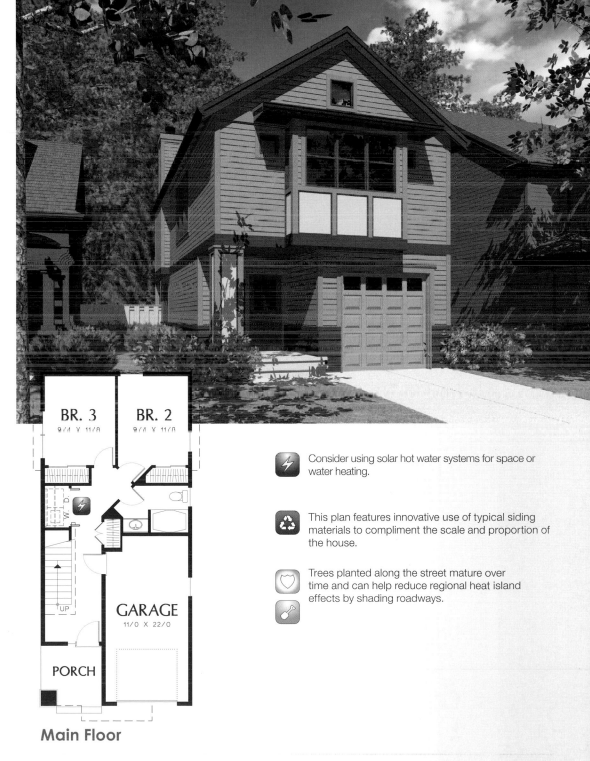

Consider using solar hot water systems for space or water heating.

This plan features innovative use of typical siding materials to compliment the scale and proportion of the house.

Trees planted along the street mature over time and can help reduce regional heat island effects by shading roadways.

MASTER
14/2 X 14/0
(9' CLG.)

MEDIA CENTER

VAULTED
GREAT RM.
15/0 X 20/4

DINING
12/0 X 12/0
(9' CLG.)

SPA

NICHE

GARAGE/
SHOP
10/0 X 17/6

11/0 X 13/0
(9' CLG.)

NICHE

DESK

REF

PANTRY

BR. 2
10/0 X 11/2
(9' CLG.)

BUILT-IN
OR CLOSET

DEN
10/2 X 12/10
(9' CLG.)

FOYER
(9' CLG.)

W D

GARAGE
20/0 X 19/6

LIN.

©Alan Mascord Design Associates, Inc.

Main Floor

Plant shade trees to keep your home cool in the summer.

Orienting your home east to west, and controlling sunlight on the south side of your home effectively uses free solar energy.

Take shorter showers or consider replacing your shower head with an ultra low-flow version.

Home Facts

Brumley
Plan G21111 Price Code **C**

Living Space	Sq Ft
Upper Floor	871
Main Floor	1,117
Total Living Space	**1,988**

Width	40'-0"
Depth	44'-0"
Bedrooms	3*
Bathrooms	2.5

* Number of rooms specifically designed for sleeping quarters. Calculation of bedrooms for certification purposes may be higher.

Efficient Living Rating

Making smart choices when building your home can save you money as well as reduce environmental impact. For example, if you feel you wouldn't use a spa tub, do not install one.

Buy rechargeable batteries to prevent items from going to the landfill.

When giving gifts for birthdays, etc., consider using a gift bag. It can be reused multiple times, preventing wrapping materials from going to the landfill. It also reduces the cost in gift-giving.

Preserving existing trees and foliage can increase the value of your property as well as maintain the environment.

Upper Floor

MASTER
VAULTED
14/0 X 12/0+/-

LINEN

DN.

OPEN TO BELOW

BR. 3
10/2 X 11/2

BR. 2
11/0 X 12/2 +

Main Floor

©Alan Mascord Design Associates, Inc.

MEDIA

DINING
11/0 X 11/0
(9' CLG.)

VAULTED
GREAT RM
16/0 X 16/0

BUILT-INS OR FURNITURE

BUILT-INS

REF PAN

STOR

W D.

GARAGE
19/0 X 21/0

UP
(11' CLG.)

BUILT-IN DESK

OFFICE
11/0 X 10/10
(9' CLG.)

Home Facts

Mallory
Plan G21118 Price Code **C**

Living Space	Sq Ft
Upper Floor	658
Main Floor	858
Total Living Space	**1,516**

Width	22'-0"
Depth	43'-0"
Bedrooms	3*
Bathrooms	2.5

* Number of rooms specifically designed for sleeping quarters. Calculation of bedrooms for certification purposes may be higher.

Efficient Living Rating

Detached garage plan available.

Please note: Photographed home may have been modified to suit home owner's preference.

Look for the Energy Star label when buying appliances and electronics.

The cedar siding chosen for this home was produced locally. Because it is a natural and locally occurring material, it is well suited to the elements.

A metal roof, as shown on the opposite page, can be used to collect rainwater for use on all plants, whereas chemicals from an asphalt roof may make it unsuitable for watering vegetables.

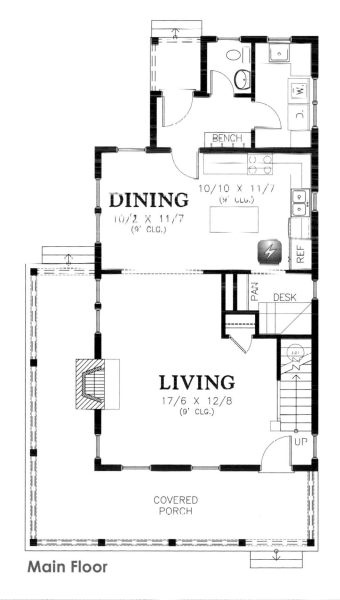

DINING
10/2 X 11/7
(9' CLG.)

10/10 X 11/7
(9' CLG.)

BENCH

PAN

DESK

LIVING
17/6 X 12/8
(9' CLG.)

UP

COVERED PORCH

Main Floor

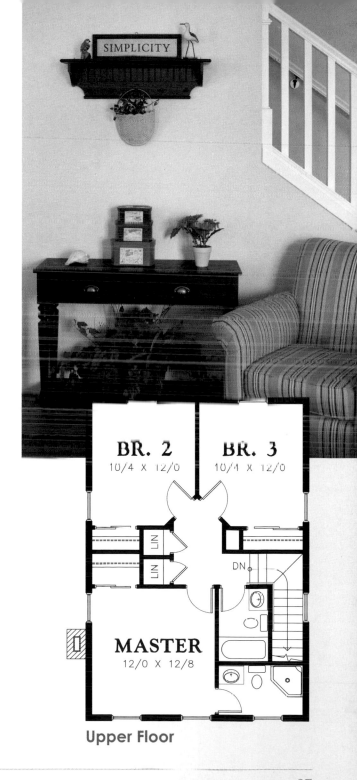

SIMPLICITY

BR. 2
10/4 X 12/0

BR. 3
10/4 X 12/0

LIN

LIN

DN

MASTER
12/0 X 12/8

Upper Floor

97

PORCH

DINING
11/2 X 12/8
(9' CLG.)

VAULTED
MASTER
12/8 X 15/2

SHELVES

BUILT-INS

VAULTED
GREAT RM.
16/8 X 17/0

11/4 X 12/10

P.

W. D.

REF.

MEDIA

LIN. LIN.

FOYER
(10' CLG.)

BR. 3/
DEN
10/6 X 11/4
(9' CLG.)

GARAGE
20/6 X 21/0

BR. 2
11/0 X 10/0
(9' CLG.)

© Alan Mascord Design Associates, Inc.

PORCH

Main Floor

 Add dimmers to lights to make them adjustable for specific tasks to reduce unnecessary energy use.

Store drinking water in the refrigerator instead of running the cold tap to get a cool drink.

Existing tree preservation retains mature trees for use as shading elements, keeping your home cool.

Home Facts

Crawford
Plan G22162 Price Code **D**

Living Space	Sq Ft
Upper Floor	1,072
Main Floor	1,028
Total Living Space	**2,100**

Width	34'-0"
Depth	45'-0"
Bedrooms	4*
Bathrooms	2.5

* Number of rooms specifically designed for sleeping quarters. Calculation of bedrooms for certification purposes may be higher.

Efficient Living Rating
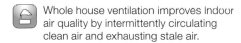

Whole house ventilation improves indoor air quality by intermittently circulating clean air and exhausting stale air.

i Help eliminate dirt from being tracked through the house by adding shoe storage near the entry.

DINING
12/6 X 11/0
(9' CLG.)

GREAT RM.
18/6 X 16/6
(9' CLG.)

MED.

BUILT-INS

15/2 X 8/10+/-
(9' CLG.)

REF PAN

UP

STOR

GARAGE
19/0 X 21/0

2 STORY
FOYER

D W

©Alan Mascord Design Associates, Inc.

Main Floor

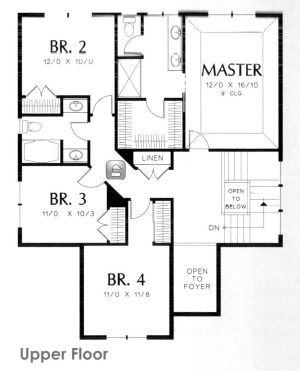

BR. 2
12/0 X 10/0

MASTER
12/0 X 16/10
9' CLG.

LINEN

BR. 3
11/0 X 10/3

OPEN
TO
BELOW

DN

BR. 4
11/0 X 11/8

OPEN
TO
FOYER

Upper Floor

See the DVD to view this kitchen in 3D, explore appliance options and to learn more about efficient living.

Only run the dishwasher when it is full to reduce water and energy consumption.

Consider purchasing items that contain recycled content.

Take advantage of daylight by using light-colored, loose-weave curtains on your windows to allow daylight to penetrate the room while preserving privacy. Also, decorate with lighter colors that reflect daylight.

Home Facts

Ackley
Plan G22145 Price Code **D**

Living Space	Sq Ft
Upper Floor	614
Main Floor	1,675
Total Living Space	**2,289**

Width	48'-0"
Depth	56'-0"
Bedrooms	3*
Bathrooms	2.5

* Number of rooms specifically designed for sleeping quarters. Calculation of bedrooms for certification purposes may be higher.

Efficient Living Rating

Main Floor

VAULTED
MASTER
15/0 X 11/8 +

SPA

MEDIA

NICHE

LINEN

VAULTED
GREAT RM.
16/0 X 17/0

NOOK
11/0 X 9/0
(9' CLG.)

UP

GARAGE
19/6 X 20/6

PAN O.

BUTLER'S PANTRY

REF

W D

SHLV

DEN
10/0 X 10/6
(9' CLG.)

DINING
11/0 X 10/2
(9' CLG.)

©Alan Mascord Design Associates, Inc.

Upper Floor

BR. 2
11/0 x 15/0

DN.

BR. 3
11/2 X 12/4

LIN

ATTIC STORAGE

©Alan Mascord Design Associates, Inc.

Home Facts

Riverton
Plan G1144B Price Code **C**

Living Space	Sq Ft
Main Floor	1,873
Total Living Space	**1,873**

Width	70'-0"
Depth	51'-0"
Bedrooms	3*
Bathrooms	2

* Number of rooms specifically designed for sleeping quarters. Calculation of bedrooms for certification purposes may be higher.

Efficient Living Rating

 See the DVD to view this kitchen in 3D, explore appliance options and to learn more about efficient living.

 This elongated plan can take advantage of passive solar principles if oriented correctly.

 Connect your irrigation system to your rainwater harvesting system to automatically use free water.

Ceiling fans can be used for comfort cooling, reducing the necessity of an air conditioning unit.

PORCH

DINING
10/6 X 13/0
(9' CLG.)

SHOP /
3RD CAR
12/6 X 19/6

MASTER
16/2 X 14/0 +
(9' CLG.)

VAULTED
GREAT RM.
17/6 X 20/6

9/6 X 15/0

PAN.

BUILT-INS

REF.

W D

GARAGE
21/0 X 22/6

DEN
11/0 X 10/0
(9' CLG.)

BR. 2
11/0 X 12/6
(9' CLG.)

BR. 3
11/2 X 12/6
(9' CLG.)

© Alan Mascord Design Associates, Inc.

Main Floor

101

Water

Water, Water Everywhere

Most of us take our drinking water for granted. We've become accustomed to getting clean, safe water whenever and wherever we might need it. For most Americans, fresh water flows freely from the faucet every time we turn it on. As a resource, however, drinking water is in alarmingly short supply. Two thirds of the planet may be covered in water, yet less than 1% of all that water is potable (suitable for drinking). Protecting fresh water resources and using them wisely is imperative to being able to continue our lifestyles.

Individually, less than 20% of the potable water we use is actually used for drinking. We use the remaining 80% for bathing, flushing our toilets, watering our gardens, doing laundry, washing dishes, cleaning our cars, and a multitude of other small tasks. According to the American Water Works Association, the average household uses 350 gallons of water a day (or approximately 127,400 gallons a year). Of this amount, toilets account for 27.7%, washing machines for 20.9%, and showers for17.3%.

In addition, all the drinking water supplied by a municipality is generally treated, pumped and routed to your home using valuable natural resources and consuming man-power and energy for each drop used. Such costs are directly passed onto consumers in the form of a utility bill.

Furthermore, the sewer systems we employ to direct waste water back to treatment plants are often compromised when linked to storm water systems that are already over their design capacity. Each time it rains, our homes are covered with water. How we deal with that water has a huge impact on our efficiency; we can direct it away from the site through the storm water system, let it soak into areas within our bounds, or we could collect and use the water appropriately – reducing our consumption of municipal water, as well as redirecting rain from the storm water system.

Indoor Water Use

Having a continuous supply of fresh, clean water is a universal desire and a worldwide need, something none of us want to do without. Other than using water for irrigation, the majority of the water we use at home is indoors. Paying careful attention to the systems we use to deliver potable water can aid in our efforts to be efficient without impacting our lifestyles.

Efficient Distribution Systems

A water efficient distribution system minimizes plumbing requirements between the water source and destination. Such components include centrally located water heat sources, wet areas in close proximity, and central manifold or recirculating plumbing systems. These elements reduce the time needed for hot water to appear at the faucet, the amount of water we waste waiting for it, and reduces the amount of energy lost in transition.

Leaks

Surprisingly, leaks can be a significant portion of your indoor water use. According to a study conducted by the American Water Works Association (AWWA), leaks make up about 14% of all indoor water use. If you have leaks, fixing them is an easy and highly effective way to save water. Check your utility bill to see if your water consumption seems realistic. If it's high, you may have a leak. One of the most common leaks is the toilet; even if there are no visible signs of water leaking from the tank to the bowl, the flapper may be faulty. To check, pour food coloring into the tank and wait a couple of hours to see if the water in the bowl changes color. If it does you have a leak and will need to change the flapper.

Photo courtesy of Whirlpool® Home Appliances

Reducing Water Consumption

After checking that your plumbing distribution system is effective and that there are no leaks, the primary way to reduce indoor water consumption is to select efficient faucets and appliances. Selecting low-flow sink faucets and showerheads, and installing efficient toilets can reduce indoor water use by 30-40%. Dual flush toilets enable occupants to select a suitable amount of water for the task, while low flow showerheads are available that reduce the amount of water consumed while maintaining comfort level and satisfaction with the shower experience. Reducing the amount of hot water we use in the shower also leads to significant energy savings. Low flow showerheads alone can save 300 lbs. of CO_2 per year for electrically heated water, or 80 pounds for gas-heated water. For household chores, make sure you select ENERGY STAR rated appliances that promote water efficiency.

Water Collection and Re-use

After you have reduced your consumption of water as much as possible, the next step is to modify the source of water. This means acquiring an alternate source of water, which can be accomplished in a couple of ways:

- Collecting rainwater (Rainwater Harvesting)
- Re-using indoor wash water (Grey Water)

Rainwater Harvesting

Rainwater harvesting sounds technical, but it doesn't need to be. Systems can be as simple as a single, simple container on the end of a downspout which collects water for lawn and garden irrigation. Systems can also be as involved as collection tanks above or below ground that store run-off from rooftops and other collection surfaces and filter it in various ways before directing it indoors for use with your washing machine, dishwasher, or toilets. More complex systems additionally incorporate filtration elements to make harvested water potable. The complexity and size of the system installed simply depends on your intent.

A small rain barrel as shown may suffice for irrigating small yard areas over short dry periods, but for larger areas or extended periods of summer, larger collection tanks may be required.

When collecting rainwater for use indoors, make sure you follow the guidelines set by the local building department. Some municipalities rely on the water in your toilet tank as an emergency drinking water source and require it to potable.

Grey Water

As well as collecting rainwater, we have the option of re-using water that has already been used indoors. Water that has been used to do your laundry or run your dishwasher is considered to be grey water—water that does not contain human waste. Re-directing grey water to a storage tank makes it available for use outdoors. It's important to point out the negative effect of using untreated, detergent filled water on your vegetable garden. Consider using eco-friendly cleaning materials, soaps and detergents when using a grey water system for irrigation. Using compatible systems will keep you, your family, and the environment safe and healthy.

Stormwater Management

With increased population and urban expansion, older storm water sewer systems are often inundated with water during and after a downpour. When the water from everybody's rooftops is directed to older, city wide sewer systems, sewers quickly reach maximum capacity and may overflow and cause flooding with human waste and contaminated water. With that in mind, it makes a good deal of preventative sense to deal with your own storm water (the water that falls on your home and garden) within the bounds of your lot. Water can be redirected and dealt with in interesting ways.

Pervious Surfaces

It's important to be conscious of rainwater run-off from driveways and walkways. These surfaces are generally made out of impervious materials such as concrete or mortared stonework, and water run-off needs to be directed somewhere, often causing problems.

To prevent run-off from hard surfaces, many products have been developed to be pervious to water while also retaining the original surface so that it continues to be suitable for driving and walking on. Appropriately installed paving stones can be used to allow water to soak into the ground between stone sections, or special concrete mixes can be used to provide a path for water through the material.

Vegetative Swales

A swale is a trough or trench that is dug and filled with drainage material and plant-life to slowly absorb rainwater into the ground during and after a downpour. Water can also be moved from one location to another by installing a perforated pipe at the bottom of the trench. Using a swale on your site reduces the impact on storm water systems.

Rain Gardens

Rain gardens offer you the chance to enjoy the rain by displacing it and using it in appropriate areas within your landscaping. Designed to collect the water and let the ground absorb it slowly, rain gardens may sport water features, basins with plants that incorporate ornamental features, or even original sculptures (as pictured). The ways in which you can enjoy the rain in your garden are limited only by your own creative impulses and the dexterity of your green thumbs. Speak to a local landscaper for more ideas and information.

Planters

Planters can add a botanical element to your landscape while managing storm water. Incorporating features from both vegetative swales and rain gardens, planters are a popular way of slowing down rainwater before it enters a sewer system.

Home Facts

Jasmine
Plan G21114 Price Code **C**

Living Space	Sq Ft
Upper Floor	817
Main Floor	1,079
Total Living Space	**1,896**
Width	28'-0"
Depth	43'-0"
Bedrooms	3*
Bathrooms	2.5

* Number of rooms specifically designed for sleeping quarters. Calculation of bedrooms for certification purposes may be higher.

Efficient Living Rating

Detached garage plan available.

Do not leave sprinklers unattended. Garden hoses can pour out 600 gallons of water in just a few hours. Use a timer to remind yourself to turn it off.

The simple foundation shape of this home reduces the materials and labor necessary to build it.

Minimal transition space equates to more usable space in a compact design.

Centrally locating the water heater and furnace will reduce the length of pipe and duct runs.

Enclosing the front porch, as shown on the home to the left, expands living space.

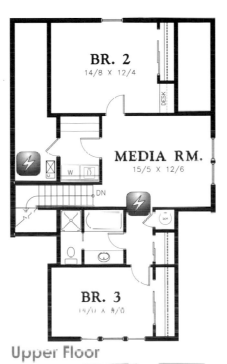

Upper Floor

BR. 2
14/8 X 12/4

MEDIA RM.
15/5 X 12/6

BR. 3
11/7 X 9/0

Main Floor

MASTER
11/3 X 13/2
(9' CLG.)

15/4 X 9/4
(9' CLG.)

DINING
13/0 X 12/0
(9' CLG.)

LIVING
15/3 X 12/11
(9' CLG.)

BENCH   PANTRY
MUDROOM

COVERED PORCH

©Alan Mascord Design Associates, Inc.

Note: Photographed homes may have been modified to suit homeowner's preference.

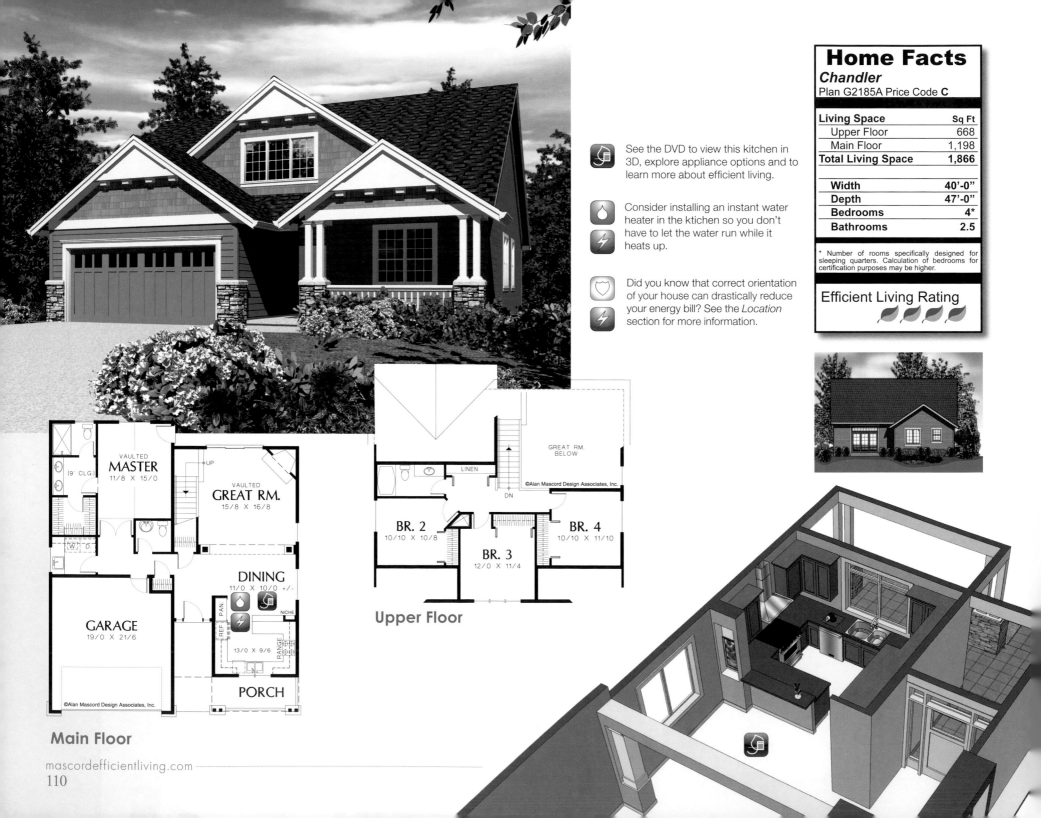

Home Facts

Chandler
Plan G2185A Price Code **C**

Living Space	Sq Ft
Upper Floor	668
Main Floor	1,198
Total Living Space	**1,866**

Width	40'-0"
Depth	47'-0"
Bedrooms	4*
Bathrooms	2.5

* Number of rooms specifically designed for sleeping quarters. Calculation of bedrooms for certification purposes may be higher.

Efficient Living Rating

See the DVD to view this kitchen in 3D, explore appliance options and to learn more about efficient living.

Consider installing an instant water heater in the ktichen so you don't have to let the water run while it heats up.

Did you know that correct orientation of your house can drastically reduce your energy bill? See the *Location* section for more information.

Main Floor

VAULTED MASTER
11/8 X 15/0
(9' CLG.)

VAULTED GREAT RM.
15/8 X 16/8

DINING
11/0 X 10/0 +/-

NICHE

REF. PAN. RANGE

13/0 X 9/6

GARAGE
19/0 X 21/6

PORCH

©Alan Mascord Design Associates, Inc.

Upper Floor

GREAT RM. BELOW

LINEN

DN

BR. 2
10/10 X 10/8

BR. 3
12/0 X 11/4

BR. 4
10/10 X 11/10

©Alan Mascord Design Associates, Inc.

Home Facts

Maysville

Plan G2201J Price Code **E**

Living Space	Sq Ft
Upper Floor	1,468
Main Floor	1,444
Total Living Space	**2,912**

Width	**50'-0"**
Depth	**59'-0"**
Bedrooms	**4***
Bathrooms	**2.5**

* Number of rooms specifically designed for sleeping quarters. Calculation of bedrooms for certification purposes may be higher.

Efficient Living Rating

Upper Floor

MASTER
VAULTED
12/0 X 15/0 +
(9' CLG.)

SPA

FAMILY RM. BELOW

BR. 4
12/2 X 11/4
(9' CLG.)

BR. 3
11/2 X 13/8 +/-
(9' CLG.)

DN.

W D

STUDY
9/6 X 10/0
(9' CLG.)

FOYER BELOW

BR. 2
VAULTED
13/0 X 11/4

©Alan Mascord Design Associates, Inc.

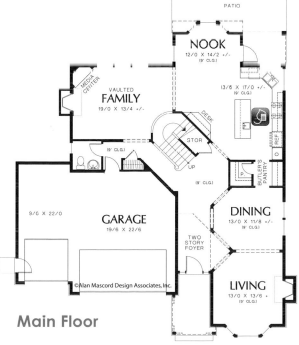

Main Floor

PATIO

NOOK
12/0 X 14/2 +/-
(9' CLG.)

FAMILY
VAULTED
19/0 X 13/4 +/-
(9' CLG.)

MEDIA CENTER

DESK

STOR

UP

BUTLER'S PANTRY

DINING
13/0 X 11/8 +/-
(9' CLG.)

GARAGE
19/6 X 22/6

9/6 X 22/0

TWO STORY FOYER

LIVING
13/0 X 13/6 +
(9' OLG.)

©Alan Mascord Design Associates, Inc.

 See the DVD to view this kitchen in 3D, explore appliance options and to learn more about efficient living.

 Check for toilet leaks by adding food coloring to the toilet tank. If there is a leak, color will appear in the bowl in 30 minutes. Flush when the test is done so the food coloring does not stain the bowl.

 Check the AC in your car regularly. Leaks can cause pollution in the environment.

 Avoid the installation of ornamental water features unless the water they use is recycled. Locate them where there is minimal loss due to evaporation.

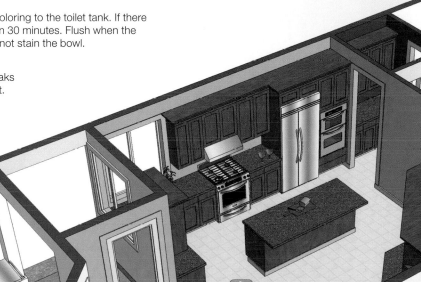

Be sure to take advantage of space under the stairs for storage.

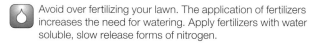

Avoid over fertilizing your lawn. The application of fertilizers increases the need for watering. Apply fertilizers with water soluble, slow release forms of nitrogen.

When adjusting water temperatures, if the water is too hot or too cold, try turning down the offending knob rather than increasing water flow in the other to compensate.

©Alan Mascord Design Associates, Inc.

Upper Floor

©Alan Mascord Design Associates, Inc.

Main Floor

Home Facts

Corbett

Plan G2154F Price Code **C**

Living Space	Sq Ft
Upper Floor	784
Main Floor	716
Total Living Space	**1,500**
Width	36'-0"
Depth	44'-0"
Bedrooms	3*
Bathrooms	2.5

* Number of rooms specifically designed for sleeping quarters. Calculation of bedrooms for certification purposes may be higher.

Efficient Living Rating

 See the DVD to view this kitchen in 3D, explore appliance options and to learn more about efficient living.

 Do not use running water to thaw meat or other frozen foods. Defrost food overnight in the refrigerator or use the defrost function on your microwave.

 Observe speed limits, accelerate smoothly and moderately, and avoid idling to reduce car emissions.

 Install a programmable thermostat or individual room thermostats to control heating and cooling equipment.

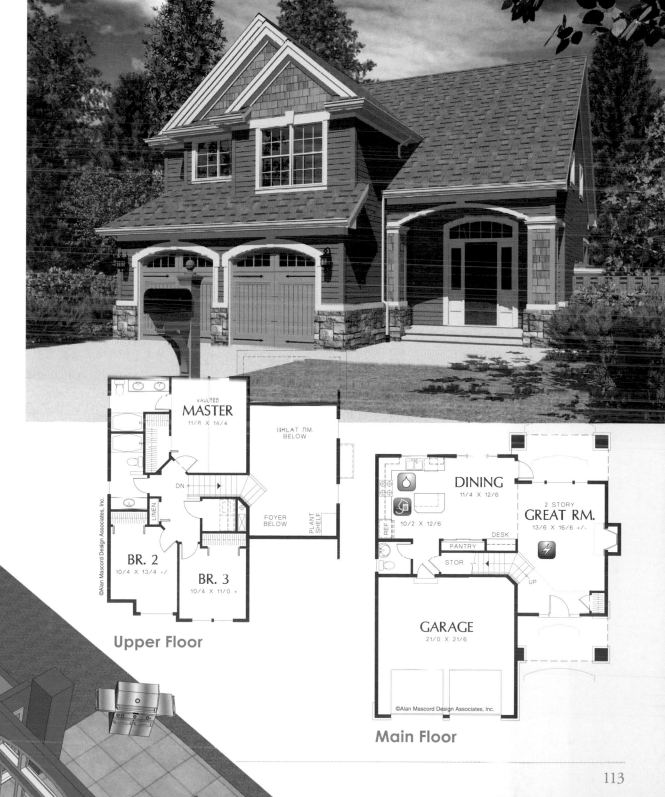

Upper Floor

Main Floor

Living Space	Sq Ft
Upper Floor	1,077
Main Floor	1,364
Total Living Space	**2,441**
Width	44'-0"
Depth	72'-0"
Bedrooms	4*
Bathrooms	2.5

* Number of rooms specifically designed for sleeping quarters. Calculation of bedrooms for certification purposes may be higher.

Efficient Living Rating

 A detached garage linked by a covered walkway allows the homeowner to isolate elements away from the clean living space.

 Clean furnace filters monthly. Dirty filters restrict air flow and increase energy use.

See the DVD to view Sketchup™ models of the exterior and kitchen of this home in 3D, explore appliance options, and to learn more about Efficient Living.

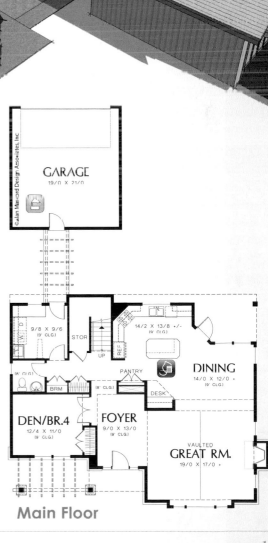

Upper Floor

Main Floor

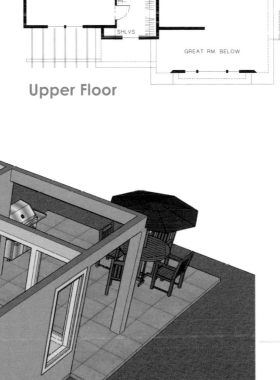

Home Facts
Summerwood
Plan G1137 Price Code **C**

Living Space	Sq Ft
Main Floor	1,632
Total Living Space	**1,632**
Bonus Room	+1,043

Width	50'-0"
Depth	50'-0"
Bedrooms	5*
Bathrooms	3

* Number of rooms specifically designed for sleeping quarters. Calculation of bedrooms for certification purposes may be higher.

Efficient Living Rating

Plan designed for daylight lot.

Using a hose to clean the driveway can waste hundreds of gallons of water. Use a broom or a leaf blower instead.

Unfinished basements offer expandable space for expanding families.

Add bins for sorting recyclables in the pantry, mudroom, or a kitchen cabinet.

Main Floor

DECK

VAULTED MASTER
14/0 X 12/8

GREAT RM.
16/0 X 16/4
(11' CLG.)

NOOK
9/0 X 9/0
(9' CLG.)

NICHE

BR. 2
11/4 X 10/0
(9' CLG.)

LINEN
SHLVS
PAN REF

DINING
11/4 X 12/2
(9' CLG.)

GARAGE
19/8 X 21/8

DEN/BR. 3
11/6 X 10/4
(9' CLG.)

PORCH

SEAT

BENCH

DN

©Alan Mascord Design Associates, Inc.

Lower Floor

FUTURE
BR. 5
10/6 X 12/8

FUTURE
BR. 4
10/4 X 12/8

FUTURE
GAMES RM.
16/0 X 16/8 +

CRAWLSPACE

UP

CRAWLSPACE

©Alan Mascord Design Associates, Inc.

Home Facts

Mansfield
Plan G22137F Price Code **E**

Living Space	Sq Ft
Upper Floor	1,571
Main Floor	1,424
Total Living Space	**2,995**
Width	35'-0"
Depth	64'-0"
Bedrooms	3*
Bathrooms	2.5

* Number of rooms specifically designed for sleeping quarters. Calculation of bedrooms for certification purposes may be higher.

Efficient Living Rating

Upper Floor

Main Floor

©Alan Mascord Design Associates, Inc.

 See the DVD to view this kitchen in 3D, explore appliance options and to learn more about efficient living.

 Avoid flushing the toilet unnecessarily. Dispose of tissues and other such waste in recycling or trash, as appropriate, rather than the toilet, and redirect your unwanted bugs to the outdoors.

 Check your refrigerator for leaky gaskets around the door to reduce cooling load on the interior. An easy way to test the gasket is by closing the door on a dollar bill. If you can't pull the bill out of the door easily, the gasket is in good shape.

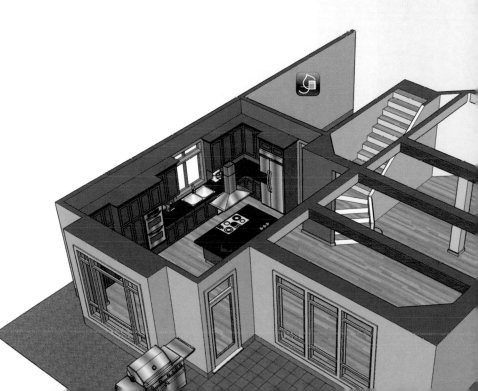

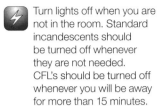

Home Facts
Anson
Plan G22109 Price Code **D**

Living Space	Sq Ft
Upper Floor	960
Main Floor	1,302
Total Living Space	**2,262**

Width	40'-0"
Depth	40'-0"
Bedrooms	3*
Bathrooms	2.5

* Number of rooms specifically designed for sleeping quarters. Calculation of bedrooms for certification purposes may be higher.

Efficient Living Rating

Plan designed for sloping lot

Turn lights off when you are not in the room. Standard incandescents should be turned off whenever they are not needed. CFL's should be turned off whenever you will be away for more than 15 minutes.

Repair dripping faucets by replacing washers. If your faucet is dripping at the rate of one drop per second, you can expect to waste 2700 gallons of water per year, adding to your utility bill and putting a strain on your septic system, if you have one.

Take advantage of your site topography. On sloping lots, garages on the lower level take advantage of otherwised unused crawlspace.

Upper Floor

Main Floor

Lower Floor

Home Facts

Granville

Plan G1103BA Price Code **C**

Living Space	Sq Ft
Main Floor	1,850
Total Living Space	**1,850**
Width	**44'-0"**
Depth	**68'-0"**
Bedrooms	**3***
Bathrooms	**2**

* Number of rooms specifically designed for sleeping quarters. Calculation of bedrooms for certification purposes may be higher.

Efficient Living Rating

DINING
10/0 X 11/4
(9' CLG.)

MASTER
12/0 X 15/4 +/-
(9' CLG.)

SHLVS

MEDIA CENTER

GREAT RM.
14/10 X 19/2 +/-
(9' CLG.)

LINEN

BR. 2
12/0 X 10/0
(9' CLG.)

10/2 X 13/10+/-
(9' CLG.)

(9' CLG.)

BR. 3
12/0 X 10/0
(9' CLG.)

REF

PAN

FOYER
(10' CLG.)

W/D

(9' CLG.)

BUILT IN

VAULTED
DEN
13/0 X 13/2+

WINDOW SEAT

GARAGE
20/0 X 21/6

©Alan Mascord Design Associates, Inc.

Main Floor

 See the DVD to view this kitchen in 3D, explore appliance options and to learn more about efficient living.

Take advantage of daylight by using light colored, loose weave curtains on your windows to allow daylight to penetrate the room while preserving privacy. Also, decorate with lighter colors that reflect daylight.

When appropriate, buy reused, refurbished or reconditioned goods rather than new.

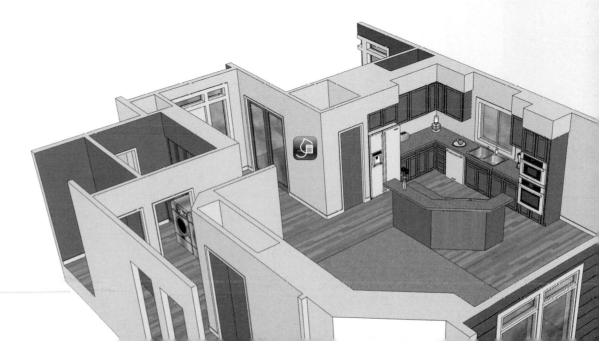

Air Quality

Take a Deep Breath

Indoor environmental quality is a deeply important factor in maintaining a healthy home. The Environmental Protection Agency (EPA) and its Science Advisory Board have consistently ranked indoor air pollution among the top five environmental risks to public health. U.S. EPA studies have shown that the levels of many airborne pollutants may be 25 to 100 times higher indoors than outdoors. Indoor environmental quality encompasses many factors and conditions, including temperature, relative humidity, airborne pollutants and a multitude of other circumstances that can affect the overall comfort and wellbeing of your family.

Indoor air pollution is one of the most prevalent, complex, and damaging obstacles a home environment can face. There are many identifiable air pollutants, including sources such as radon gas, mold, and combustion sources such as oil, gas, kerosene, coal, wood and tobacco products. Many things we use to construct our homes may also contain pollutants that compromise the safety of our families, such as substances found in certain adhesives, carpet, flooring, paint, cabinetry or furniture, etc. During our time at home, we can also personally contribute to indoor pollution by choosing to use certain products. Such items include contaminating products used for household cleaning and maintenance, personal care, or hobbies.

Poor indoor air quality is a significant cause of comfort and health problems. Among high-risk individuals (the very young, the elderly, and the chronically ill), poor air quality can lead to very serious health problems. Radon, chemicals, and outdoor air pollution can cause asthma, skin irritation, allergies, and major medical problems, as serious as cancer.

To prevent or minimize the comfort or health problems associated with indoor air quality we need to become educated about what we can do to keep our air clean, ventilate our living spaces, control dust, prevent mold, and minimize our use of potentially harmful (and toxic) products and chemicals.

Cleaning the Air

Ventilation and Air Filtration

To be efficient, we need to prevent uncontrolled air movement in and out of the home. We pay to condition the air inside our homes, and uncontrolled loss means extra costs re-conditioning replacement air. Instead, we want to seal the envelope tightly and control ventilation properly.

As with an automobile engine, you don't want oil to leak out of its own accord before you replace it with fresh oil; you want to control when you empty and change it. Of course, making sure the air in your home is adequate and clean is as important as making sure your car has enough clean oil to run smoothly.

An HVAC professional can properly calculate the amount of air required for ventilation in your home. This professional will take into account all the variables associated with properly sizing ventilation equipment; the number of bathroom and kitchen fans, regional air pressure, size of your indoor spaces, and your selection of heating equipment, to name a few.

To maintain adequate fresh air, your HVAC professional may recommend a whole house ventilation system (with Heat Recovery) to change the air within your home regularly. This ensures that you always breathe fresh air while maintaining a high level of energy efficiency, exchanging energy from outgoing air to incoming air.

The air we use to ventilate our homes comes from the outside, and is subjected to external pollutants before we use it. Consider filtering the air your system uses to protect your family from airborn pollutants. There are various types of air filters including MERV filters and HEPA filters.

MERV, or Minimum Efficiency Reporting Value, refers to the filtration efficiency of an air filter that has undergone a standard test procedure. Performance is determined by comparing airborne particle counts upstream and downstream of the air filter. HEPA, or High Efficiency Particle Arresting, filters are rigorously designed to capture particles: in fact, HEPA filters are 99.97% effective in capturing particles as small as 0.3 microns. It is important to confirm that all your HVAC equipment is compatible.

Controlling Dust

While preventing the build-up of dust may not completely reduce asthmatic or allergic symptoms, controlling dust is one of the most proactive measures you can take in keeping your interior environment healthy. Below are a few examples of simple steps you can take to control the amount of dust that accumulates within your house:

- Provide shoe storage at entrances for homeowners and visitors. Removing your shoes at the door prevents tracking dust further into your home.

- Install a special high-efficiency particulate air (HEPA) filter in your air conditioner or air purifier. This can help remove some allergens (such as pollen or animal dander) and tobacco smoke from the air in your home.

- Where possible, limit carpet, upholstered furniture, and heavy drapes that collect dust. Upholstry and drapes should be made from a tight weave fabric that keeps out dust.

- Use hard surfaced furniture that you can wipe clean.

- Remove wall-to-wall carpeting. Use smaller rugs (throw rugs, area rugs) that you can clean and wash more easily.

- Replace drapes and blinds with roll-down shades or washable curtains.

- Damp-mop tile and hard surfaced floors rather than sweeping. Use a washable cloth, instead of disposable wipe.

- If possible, use a central vacuum system (which vents directly outdoors). If a central vacuum is not an option, make sure to use a vacuum cleaner with a HEPA filter or a special double-thickness bag, which collects dust-mite particles and pollen. Standard paper bag filters may allow the stirred-up allergens to escape back into the room.

- Consider wet-vacuum cleaning when possible. This can help remove allergens from carpeting as it actually washes the carpet. Also, consider steam-cleaning carpets when possible. In addition to cleaning the carpet, the heat of the steam kills dust mites.

- Remember: dusting and vacuuming stir up dust, making the air worse until the dust settles. Wear a mask if you do the cleaning yourself. If possible, try to have someone without allergies do the cleaning.

Mold Prevention

Too much exposure to mold may cause or worsen conditions like asthma, hay fever, or other allergies. The most common symptoms of overexposure are cough, congestion, runny nose, eye irritation, and aggravation of asthma. Depending on the amount of exposure and a person's individual vulnerability, more serious health effects, like fevers and breathing problems, can occur.

Mold is most likely to grow where moisture is trapped in improperly ventilated spaces such as damp crawlspaces, misty bathrooms and defective wall systems. Because mold increases with humidity, it is vital that we are cognizant of areas that may trap humidity.

The key to preventing mold from forming is to prevent weather from intruding the building envelope and control the humidity inside our homes. In the construction of an energy efficient home, the exterior building envelope is designed to be air and water tight, and air movement is controlled. To ensure that any wet part of your home dries properly, it is important to include systems to supply proper ventilation throughout your home, including the building envelope and interior spaces. Examples of systems employed to help prevent water intrusion and mold growth include: drainage planes behind exterior finishes (rainscreens), properly sealed building envelopes (flashing, caulking, moisture barrier) the use of moisture resistant building materials (green board), and ventilation fans in interior spaces (Heat Recovery Ventilators, bath fans).

Volatile Organic Compounds

VOCs are Volatile Organic Compounds. Chemicals contained in the items used in the construction of our homes can emit pollutants throughout the lifespan of the product. Some sources, such as building materials, furnishings, and household products, release pollutants more or less continuously. Consider using products that contain low or no VOC.

Items to be particularly wary of include paint, caulks, sealants, cabinet materials, plastics and carpets. Reducing the amount of VOCs present improves the indoor air quality of the home, and reduces the exposure to toxic compounds.

There are healthier alternatives to traditional paints. You can achieve the same color, texture, sheen and quality of finish with VOC free paint. Look for the GreenSeal™ and ask your paint supplier about the VOC content.

PVC (Polyvinyl Chloride) is a widely used building material found in such products as window frames, flooring, and shower units. Despite appearing to be an ideal building material, studies have shown that PVC has high environmental and health costs. Where possible, think about alternatives such as wood framed windows, natural flooring materials, plumbing pipes and tiled showers.

When buying or building cabinets, specify board products that contain a urea-formaldehyde free binder. Urea-formaldehyde, found in many engineered wood products has been classified as a Toxic Air Contaminant by the California Air Resources Board due to its potential to cause cancer.

Water-based wood finishes, such as waterborne urethane or acrylic have decreased toxic compounds, while still providing comparable durability to their standard counterparts.

Clean and Green

Many cleaning products for the home also emit synthetic chemicals, VOCs, and irritating fragrances. These substances can have serious health repercussions for humans, pets and the environment. Each time you use a chemical in your home, you and your family are exposed to its harmful side effects. Not only do we absorb the chemicals during initial use - but in addition, our environment absorbs those that we dispose of.

Considering that Americans spend 90% of their time indoors, cleaning their homes with natural products is a huge step towards making your home a healthy place

Some commonly found substances in household cleaning items include:

- Artificial Fragrances - can interfere with breathing, cause skin irritation, and some even contain phthalates, which have been found to a carcinogen in lab experiments.

- Alkyphenol ethoxylates - used in detergents, has been found to be a hormone disrupter.

- Butyl cellosolve - a common degreaser that can cause nausea, headaches and more serious issues when inhaled.

- Petroleum - frequently found in conventional cleansers and soaps is flammable and releases unwanted fumes.

Wheatboard cabinets, marmoleum floor tiles and a concrete countertop provide stylish materials without emitting VOCs.

Clean and Green Alternatives

Many companies make cleaning products containing natural cleaning elements that can be found at grocery stores. Look for products that use plant oils, grain alcohols and natural fragrances. A good test is to read the label: you should be able to recognize all the ingredients. There are also some natural elements you can use as cleaning agents yourself:

• Vinegar and water can be used to clean bathrooms and windows.

• Baking Soda can replace toxic abrasive chemicals to clean toilets, tubs and sinks.

• Citrus Oils can replace artificial fragrances to freshen a room without overpowering the air.

Toxin free cleaning products are usually biodegradable and will not pollute the air or water. Cleaning with natural alternatives will reduce your exposure to toxins as well as protecting the environment.

Radon

Radon is a cancer-causing, natural radioactive gas that permeates from the ground causing concern if it leaches beneath your home. Radon is invisible to sight, smell and taste. Radon is the leading cause of lung cancer among non-smokers and is the second leading cause of lung cancer in America. It claims about 20,000 lives annually; high levels can pose a serious threat to you and your family's health.

Because radon permeates from the ground, different areas carry various levels of risk due to variations in geology. In terms of the home building process, techniques may vary for different foundation types and site requirements. The basic common elements for radon build-up prevention include: A gas permeable layer that is placed beneath the slab or flooring system to allow the soil gas to move freely beneath the house. In many cases, the material used is a 4-inch layer of clean gravel. Plastic sheeting on top of the gas permeable layer prevents the soil gas from entering the home. A 3- or 4-inch gas-tight vent pipe (commonly used for plumbing) runs from the gas permeable layer through the house and ultimately through the roof or exterior wall. This safely vents radon and other soil gases above the house. An electrical junction box can be installed in case an electric venting fan is needed later.

Consult a professional or the Environmental Protection Agency (www.epa.gov) for information on the radon risk levels in your area and appropriate techniques.

Mudrooms and shoe-storage areas provide solutions to contain dust and dirt, improving indoor air quality.

Sealing Your Home from the Garage

For a variety of reasons and personal desires, many home plans include an attached garage that is incorporated into the structure of the home. An attached garage certainly promises convenience: it keeps you dry as you come and go and guarantees an ease of transportation when moving items from the car to the home. An attached garage can allow for a more compact building footprint in places where space is a premium.

While such features add expediency to your lifestyle, there also might be some items inside the garage that need to be isolated from your family. Chemicals, paints, oils and cleaning substances usually stored in the garage attribute to air quality concerns if they leak. Your gasoline powered car emits dangerous gases while the engine is running, leaving or entering the garage.

It is vital, in the case of an attached garage, to prevent dangerous substances (such as carbon monoxide gases) from entering the home. To do so, remember to seal any gaps in walls that the home shares with the garage. Also install a CO_2 monitor in any room adjacent to the garage to warn you of problems, and consider installing a fan attached to the garage door opener to vent the garage when you leave.

Mechanical Systems and Your Garage

A special note on mechanical systems and ductwork: mechanical systems in your garage can pull air from places you don't want it to and push the air around your house. When possible, make sure to avoid the placement of ductwork or mechanical equipment in the garage to prevent toxins from entering your HVAC system. Doing so also saves energy, since any loss from the system is to the indoors, where it is needed.

Detached Garages

Detaching the garage altogether is the surest and safest measure to stop gas and chemicals from entering your home. Many of the homes in this collection feature detached garages with various plans and design options to ensure a wide array of choices.

Home Facts

Newport

Plan G21117 Price Code **B**

Living Space	Sq Ft
Upper Floor	503
Main Floor	572
Total Living Space	**1,075**
Width	**18'-0"**
Depth	**34'-0"**
Bedrooms	**2***
Bathrooms	**2.5**

* Number of rooms specifically designed for sleeping quarters. Calculation of bedrooms for certification purposes may be higher.

Efficient Living Rating

Detached garage plan available

Dual-flush toilets reduce water consumption by allowing residents to choose an appropriate amount for the task.

The long, simple rooflines of this home make an ideal location for solar panels.

Beyond reducing your carbon footprint, consider ways to become carbon positive.

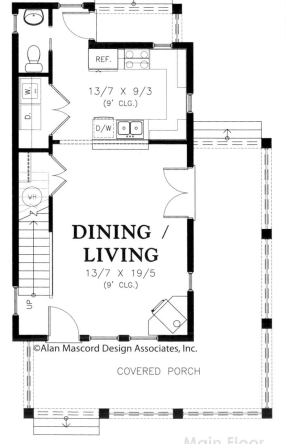

VAULTED
BR. 2
10/7 X 10/3

LINEN

LINEN   STOR.

DN.

VAULTED
BR. 1
13/7 X 10/9

Upper Floor

13/7 X 9/3
(9' CLG.)

REF.

W.

D.

D/W

WH

UP

DINING / LIVING
13/7 X 19/5
(9' CLG.)

©Alan Mascord Design Associates, Inc.

COVERED PORCH

Main Floor

Home Facts

Hemingway
Plan G22172D Price Code **E**

Living Space	Sq Ft
Top Floor	705
Upper Floor	901
Main Floor	1100
Total Living Space	**2,706**
Width	30'-0"
Depth	40'-0"
Bedrooms	3*
Bathrooms	3.5

* Number of rooms specifically designed for sleeping quarters. Calculation of bedrooms for certification purposes may be higher.

Efficient Living Rating

i This plan takes advantage of otherwise unused attic space for a large game room.

♺ See page 45 to view an elevation of this home using alternate siding materials.

COVERED PORCH

BENCH

BRM

REF

12/4 X 13/11 +/−
(9' CLG.)

6/6 X 4/0
ISLAND

DINING
16/4 X 13/10
(9' CLG.)

DESK

PAN

LIVING
16/7 X 16/10 +/−
(9' CLG.)

UP

FOYER

©Alan Mascord Design Associates, Inc.

Main Floor

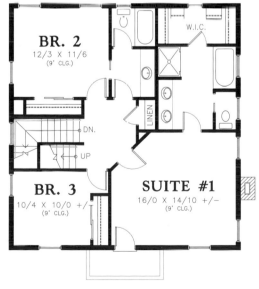

BR. 2
12/3 X 11/6
(9' CLG.)

W.I.C.

LINEN

DN.

UP

BR. 3
10/4 X 10/0 +/−
(9' CLG.)

SUITE #1
16/0 X 14/10 +/−
(9' CLG.)

Upper Floor

i

GAME ROOM
19/4 X 20/4 +/−

DN.

RAILING

Top Floor

See the DVD to view this kitchen in 3D, explore appliance options and to learn more about efficient living.

Use low or no-VOC adhesives and caulk to protect indoor air quality.

Choose a site that is located near public transportation. Using this form of transportaion can reduce emissions and toxins that cause air pollution.

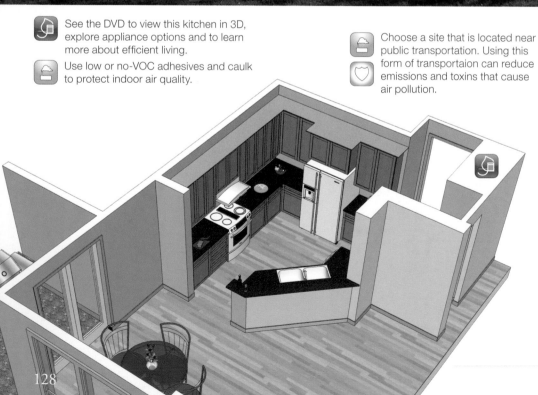

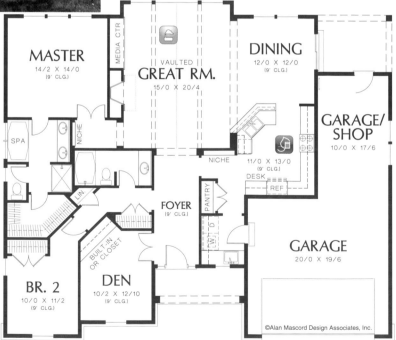

MASTER
14/2 X 14/0
(9' CLG.)

MEDIA CTR

VAULTED
GREAT RM.
15/0 X 20/4

DINING
12/0 X 12/0
(9' CLG.)

GARAGE/
SHOP
10/0 X 17/6

SPA

NICHE

NICHE

11/0 X 13/0
(9' CLG.)

DESK

REF

LIN

FOYER
(9' CLG.)

PANTRY

W D

BUILT-IN
OR CLOSET

GARAGE
20/0 X 19/6

BR. 2
10/0 X 11/2
(9' CLG.)

DEN
10/2 X 12/10
(9' CLG.)

©Alan Mascord Design Associates, Inc.

Main Floor

Home Facts

Fairfield
Plan G22159 Price Code **D**

Living Space	Sq Ft
Upper Floor	851
Main Floor	1,379
Total Living Space	**2,230**
Width	40'-0"
Depth	56'-0"
Bedrooms	3*
Bathrooms	2.5

* Number of rooms specifically designed for sleeping quarters. Calculation of bedrooms for certification purposes may be higher.

Efficient Living Rating

 See the DVD to view this kitchen in 3D, explore appliance options and to learn more about efficient living.

 Enclosed areas between living spaces and entries trap dirt and prevent it from tracking into the house.

There is a common misconception that computer screen savers save energy. They do not. Turn off the computer and/or monitor to reduce energy consumption.

Main Floor

Upper Floor

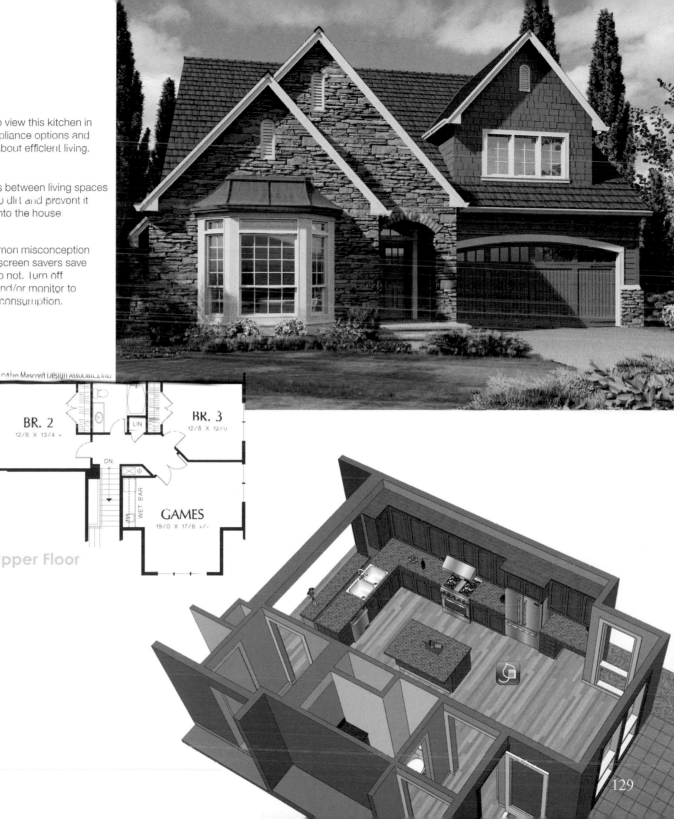

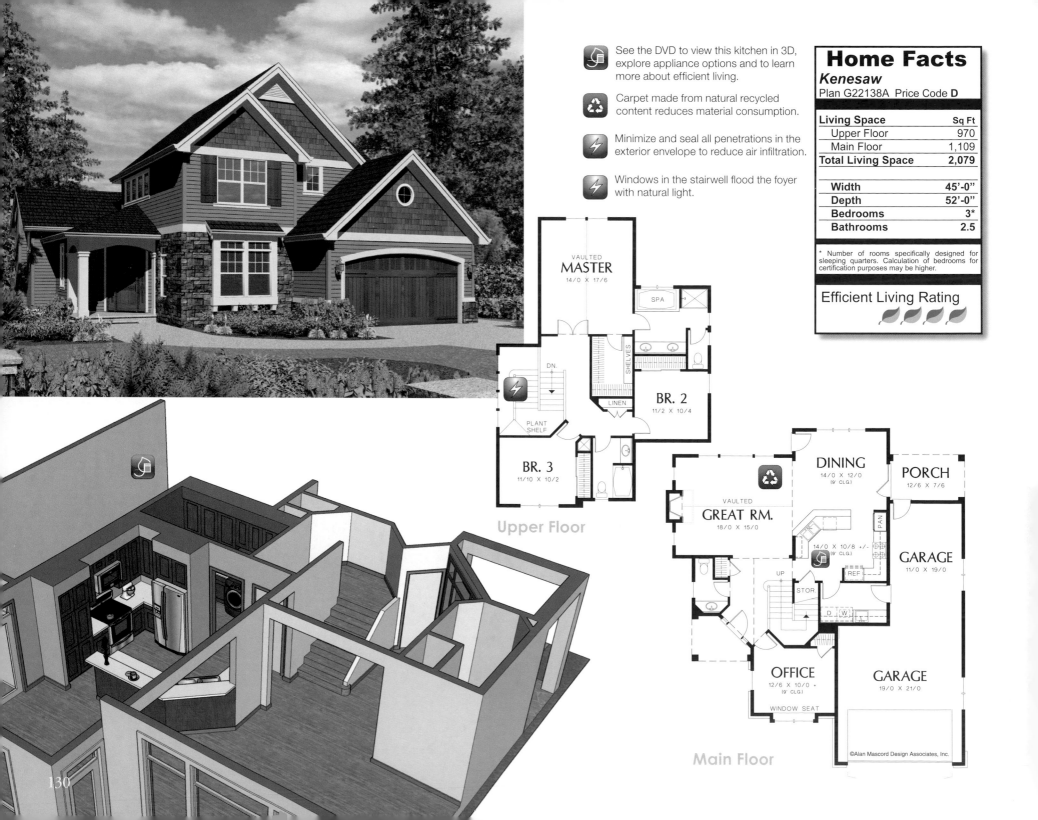

See the DVD to view this kitchen in 3D, explore appliance options and to learn more about efficient living.

Carpet made from natural recycled content reduces material consumption.

Minimize and seal all penetrations in the exterior envelope to reduce air infiltration.

Windows in the stairwell flood the foyer with natural light.

Home Facts

Kenesaw
Plan G22138A Price Code **D**

Living Space	Sq Ft
Upper Floor	970
Main Floor	1,109
Total Living Space	**2,079**

Width	45'-0"
Depth	52'-0"
Bedrooms	3*
Bathrooms	2.5

* Number of rooms specifically designed for sleeping quarters. Calculation of bedrooms for certification purposes may be higher.

Efficient Living Rating

VAULTED
MASTER
14/0 X 17/6

SPA

DN.

SHELVES

BR. 2
11/2 X 10/4

LINEN

PLANT SHELF

BR. 3
11/10 X 10/2

Upper Floor

DINING
14/0 X 12/0
(9' CLG.)

PORCH
12/6 X 7/6

VAULTED
GREAT RM.
18/0 X 15/0

PAN

14/0 X 10/8 +/-
(9' CLG.)

GARAGE
11/0 X 19/0

REF

UP

STOR.

D W

OFFICE
12/6 X 10/0 +
(9' CLG.)

GARAGE
19/0 X 21/0

WINDOW SEAT

©Alan Mascord Design Associates, Inc.

Main Floor

130

Home Facts

Landon
Plan G22140 Price Code **D**

Living Space	Sq Ft
Upper Floor	993
Main Floor	1,171
Total Living Space	**2,164**
Width	45'-0"
Depth	49'-0"
Bedrooms	3*
Bathrooms	2.5

* Number of rooms specifically designed for sleeping quarters. Calculation of bedrooms for certification purposes may be higher.

Efficient Living Rating

 See the DVD to view this kitchen in 3D, explore appliance options and to learn more about efficient living.

 Use outdoor lights with a photocell or motion sensor so they only turn on at night or when someone is present.

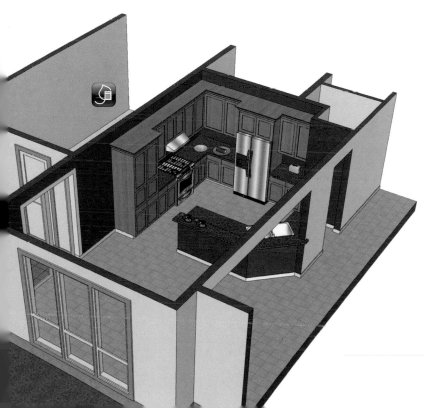

Main Floor

Upper Floor

Landscaping

Your Own Eco-System

The eco system around us is both important to our lifestyles and fragile. Site disturbance from construction practices unbalance the local system in ways that, perhaps, are not apparent at first glance. Seemingly minor changes that we make can have a large impact both locally and regionally.

Clearing landscape for construction causes problems with the management of storm water, dust, and erosion. The site itself can become unstable; landslides can occur if the ground becomes saturated and cannot deal with storm water. In addition, local storm water systems can be inundated with run off containing dust, debris, and silt.

Plants imported for landscaping may not blend with local conditions, causing the homeowner unnecessary maintenance costs or proving to be invasive. Plant species introduced into areas where they are not native can negatively impact local species. A strong invasive species could eradicate a more delicate native species, possibly removing a food source for local wildlife.

Care is needed when working with the site to prevent unnecessary disturbance to local systems, and to reduce costs associated with clearing and re-landscaping areas. Mature plants are well established, and will need less attention than freshly planted seedlings.

A well-designed, climate-appropriate landscape offers substantial environmental and economical benefits. Trees and other vegetation control erosion, protect water supplies, provide food and habitat for wildlife, and clean the air. In addition, planting trees, shrubs, bushes and hedges can be an effective way to provide shade and reduce your heating and cooling costs. Parallel to understanding how your landscape works as an eco system, approach your landscape with its unique visual appeal in mind. The sights, textures, and scents of your home's landscape might prove to be the most beautiful and inspiring of all your home's efficient features.

Shading

Using landscape shade properly requires you to understand the size, shape, and location of the moving shadow that your landscaping elements cast throughout the year, and as they mature.

Landscaping elements can be used to block sun from windows and shade your walls and walkways from hot summer rays; providing a method to reduce the cooling needs of your home.

Trees can be selected with appropriate sizes, densities, and shapes for almost any shading application. Deciduous trees, for example, can be utilized and planted to block solar heat in the summer and let more heat in during the winter. The properties of dense evergreen trees or shrubs, on the other hand, provide continuous shade and additionally serve to disperse winds.

Shading and evapotranspiration (the process by which a plant actively moves and releases water vapor) from trees reduces surrounding air temperatures by as much as 9°F. Because cool air settles near the ground, air temperatures directly under trees can be as much as 25°F cooler than air temperatures above.

Xeriscaping

Xeriscaping is a term for low-water use landscaping, while designing using native plants is called Naturescaping. Xeriscape gardens have typically been implemented in areas of the country where there is a hot-dry climate. However, busy homeowners everywhere are finding the ease of a low-maintenance garden appealing. Xeriscaping and Naturescaping reduce the need for watering, weeding, fertilizing, and spreading chemicals in our gardens.

Xeriscape design doesn't need to consist of cactus like plants, rocks and bark dust. Good design concentrates on locating plants where the species will thrive naturally and using defined areas of irrigation for water conservation rather than eliminating water use altogether. Mixing drought tolerant plants with well chosen areas of irrigated plants can produce a beautifully colored and varied garden, with a low maintenance and water requirement. For example, instead of a large lawn expanse with a high volume sprinkler system, use a smaller lawn, bordered with drought tolerant plants. Add a side flower bed planted with well chosen species using an appropriately sized irrigation system. This provides a much more interesting landscape with a colorful array of flowers while using a lot less water – with less maintenance.

Naturescaping

Since they have evolved over time to be tolerant to their surroundings, the use of native plants in your landscape can also balance the eco-system of the garden. They can provide correct nutrients to balance the soil, provide food for local wildlife, prevent the intrusive behavior of weeds and also prevent erosion.

However, you don't need to limit yourself to native

plants when planning your landscape design. Irises, Roses, Lavender, Lambs' Ears, Oriental poppy, Dusty Miller, and Tulips are all examples of plants that should survive in a low maintenance garden without overpowering native species wherever they are. The greatest pleasure of having a xeriscaped and naturescaped garden is being able to enjoy the landscape without spending too much time mowing, pruning, weeding and fertilizing.

Hydrozoning

Hydro zoning involves arranging flowers and plants into areas that need similar amounts of water and nutrients. Watering requirements are more easily managed if plants can be placed in defined areas of foliage with similar needs. Keeping thirsty plants away from your house also prevents you from needing to soak the foundation wall when watering, an often overlooked but quite problematic gardening issue.

Irrigation

If you use an automatic irrigation system, make sure to install smart, programmable sprinkler systems with moisture sensors that allow you to measure the amount of water your garden needs at any given time. Typically these systems also allow you to control irrigation from a central shut-off valve. Include a reliable rain sensor so you don't end up making the embarrassing and wasteful mistake of watering your garden in the middle of a downpour. Combine this system with a rain and wastewater collection system to maximize efficiency.

In line with naturescaping practices, it's wise to choose landscaping elements that are appropriate to the local climate and require minimal additional water. Because of their varying root systems, grass, trees, and flowers all have different water requirements. When you design your garden, consider the layout of the irrigation system, and try to group plants according to the amount of water they will need.

Know Your Bugs

Not all insects need eradicating. As every avid gardener knows, bugs can actually be beneficial and are often an essential part of your garden's eco-system. However, if your eco-system is unbalanced and there are not active 'good' bugs present, you might receive a pest infestation.

If you think you have insect pests in your garden, determine if they are actually damaging your plants beyond repair; most plants easily survive losing more than 25% of their leaf surface. Rest assured: a little damage won't hurt; if the soil is healthy, many plants outgrow the pests or diseases that afflict them. It's important to note that there may be a delay between the initial damage caused by pests and the arrival of beneficial insects that will control them. To determine if an insect is a pest or a beneficial addition to your landscape's eco-system, you might refer to gardening books or take a sample to a nursery/garden center that has a knowledgeable staff.

Pesticides

The pesticides or fertilizers you use on your garden inherently end up in the water system. Since many pesticides are highly toxic to fish and other aquatic life, even a small amount can be harmful. Worse still, the chain continues. If the fish served on your dinner plate had ingested pesticides, you will ingest them as well.

If you determine that a pest or disease problem requires intervention, make sure to use the safest method possible. There are many ways to control pests without using pesticides. Set up covers for vegetables, put out traps for slugs, and remove aphids (with water jets) while watering your plants.

Building Healthy Soil

Healthy soil is the foundation for thriving plants and a healthy lawn. Healthy plants naturally resist diseases and pests, and therefore require less care. Adding organic material improves drainage and provides food to the microscopic creatures that, in turn, provide nutrients to your plants. Add two to three inches of compost or aged manure every year by turning it into the soil (reusing it as mulch around plants).

Working Your Yard

A landscape designed for aesthetic enjoyment is a wonderful place to start. On top of their visual appeals, your yard and garden can also serve more functional, active purposes to enhance your culinary efforts. You might consider designating a section of your yard space for planting herbs, spices, fruits and vegetables that will pay back over time by reducing the amount of produce you need to buy (and nothing is more organic than retrieving cooking ingredients from your backyard). You may not have the time or inclination to delve too deeply into gardening, but consider starting out with a few simple herbs. You might be amazed by how quickly your garden matures and becomes sustainable. Of course, be mindful of any chemicals or water you use to help your produce grow. Everything the plant absorbs will be present in the fruit of your labor.

This pergola is not only an attractive architectural element and focal point for the garden, it also provides shade for south facing doors and windows to reduce heat-gain and air conditioning costs.

Copper Falls
Plan G2458

Natural Grace

Elegant, simple lines and energy-conscious finishes create a natural air in this Craftsman-inspired home, built by Lockie Homes for the Seattle Street of Dreams. Retaining the sturdy structural design and unalloyed materials revered in the craftsman style, our Copper Falls plan resonates with natural grace. Diligent consideration has been placed upon selecting eco-friendly materials and maintaining the highest possible indoor air/water quality, ensuring that this home's environmental impact will remain as clean as its lines suggest.

The home's 50-year siding and 40-year roofing materials reveal that quality of construction begins on the outside and continues within. You'll find finely-crafted details peppered throughout the interior, such as vaulted ceilings (in the great room, bonus room, and outdoor living space), generous built-ins, and a dramatic stone fireplace.

The free flowing floor plan offers an abundant amount of space while materials foster a cozy feel. Inside, deep, warm and reflective woods have been placed alongside specialty tile, granite and marble. Paperstone™, Ice Stone® and Vetrazzo® countertops (all made from post-consumer recycled content) have been utilized wherever possible. Built-in cabinetry, wood paneling, and stunning molding in the kitchen, dining room and den compliment the gorgeous flooring, composed of Forest Stewardship Council™ (FSC) certified Eco-Timber® and Treadlight™ wood (harvested from small diameter trees). Where wood has not been installed, this home features environmentally friendly flooring alternatives such as cork, wool carpet, and extraordinarily handsome tile (found in the master bath).

Whether it is at dusk, dawn, or during a rapturous orange sunset, large, well-appointed windows beckon the light inside through high-efficiency panes. An emphasis on energy and quality doesn't stop there. Low-flow toilets, ENERGY STAR rated appliances, framing with mold protection, and a Metlund® on-demand recirculation hot water system work

Photography ©Bob Greenspan

139

Well-appointed windows flood the room with natural daylight through high-efficiency panes.

to maintain clean air and conserve water. Outside, an Eco-Stone® pervious driveway and groundwater recharge system continue the home's effort towards efficiency.

Built to curb environmental impact, the Copper Falls home emphasizes classic beauty. While its splendor blossoms from basic materials and design, there's certainly nothing basic about Copper Falls. In this warm and comfortable Craftsman refuge, coming home is an embrace to you and to the environment.

141

Tall French doors optimize natural ventilation to reduce heating and cooling loads on temperate days and refresh indoor air quality.

142

Home Facts

Copper Falls
Plan G2458 Price Code **H**

Living Space	Sq Ft
Upper Floor	1,539
Main Floor	2,833
Total Living Space	**4,372**
Width	**68'-6"**
Depth	**102'-0"**
Bedrooms	**4***
Bathrooms	**4.5**

* Number of rooms specifically designed for sleeping quarters. Calculation of bedrooms for certification purposes may be higher.

Efficient Living Rating

Mulching conserves water by preventing it from evaporating out of the soil.

Donating or selling unwanted items keeps them out of the landfill.

Compost waste from your yard, as well as food items like apple cores and coffee grounds, to use as fertilizer for your garden.

When buying a new computer, remember that laptop computers consume less energy than their desktop counterparts.

Overhead pergolas at the front of this home allow daylight to further penetrate into the dining room and office while still maintaining a pleasantly scaled front porch.

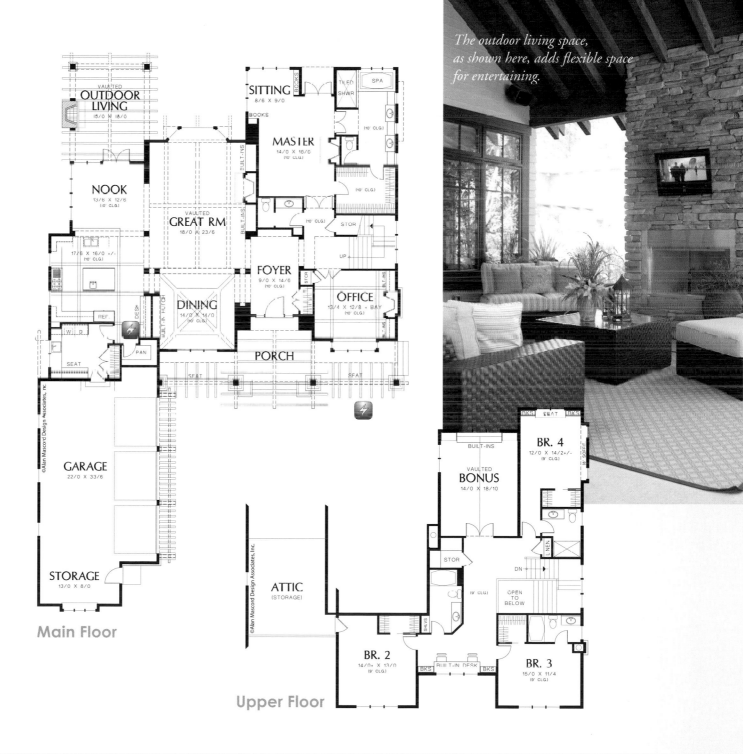

The outdoor living space, as shown here, adds flexible space for entertaining.

Main Floor

OUTDOOR LIVING
15/0 x 18/0

NOOK
13/6 x 12/6
(10' CLG.)

GREAT RM
18/0 x 23/6

SITTING
8/6 x 9/0

MASTER
14/0 x 18/0
(10' CLG.)

17/8 x 16/0 +/-
(10' CLG.)

DINING
14/0 x 14/0
(10' CLG.)

FOYER
9/0 x 14/6
(10' CLG.)

OFFICE
13/4 x 12/8 + BAY
(10' CLG.)

PORCH

GARAGE
22/0 x 33/6

STORAGE
13/0 x 8/0

©Alan Mascord Design Associates, Inc.

Upper Floor

ATTIC
(STORAGE)

BONUS
14/0 x 18/10

BR. 4
12/0 x 14/2 +/-
(9' CLG.)

BR. 2
14/0+ x 13/0
(9' CLG.)

BR. 3
15/0 x 11/4
(9' CLG.)

OPEN TO BELOW

©Alan Mascord Design Associates, Inc.

Home Facts

Malone
Plan G2164A Price Code **C**

Living Space	Sq Ft
Upper Floor	871
Main Floor	1,072
Total Living Space	**1,943**
Bonus Room	+356
Width	**40'-0"**
Depth	**52'-0"**
Bedrooms	**3***
Bathrooms	**2.5**

* Number of rooms specifically designed for sleeping quarters. Calculation of bedrooms for certification purposes may be higher.

Efficient Living Rating

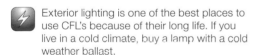

 Clean the lint filter in your dryer to improve efficiency and lengthen the life of the machine.

 Outfit your hose with a shut off valve in the spout so water only flows as needed. When finished, turn it off at the faucet to avoid leaks.

Exterior lighting is one of the best places to use CFL's because of their long life. If you live in a cold climate, buy a lamp with a cold weather ballast.

In this plan, to conserve floor area, the powder bath was tucked underneath the stairs.

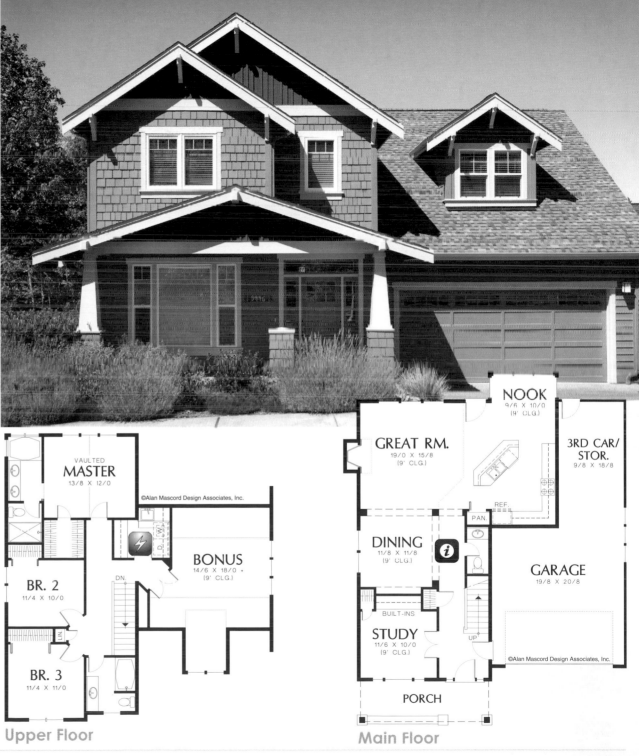

©Alan Mascord Design Associates, Inc.

VAULTED
MASTER
13/8 X 12/0

BR. 2
11/4 X 10/0

BR. 3
11/4 X 11/0

BONUS
14/6 X 18/0 +
(9' CLG.)

DN.

Upper Floor

NOOK
9/6 X 10/0
(9' CLG.)

GREAT RM.
19/0 X 15/8
(9' CLG.)

3RD CAR/
STOR.
9/8 X 18/8

REF.

PAN.

DINING
11/8 X 11/8
(9' CLG.)

GARAGE
19/8 X 20/8

BUILT-INS

STUDY
11/6 X 10/0
(9' CLG.)

UP

©Alan Mascord Design Associates, Inc.

PORCH

Main Floor

Innovative Sustainable Solutions from Whirlpool Corporation

KitchenAid® Brand

KitchenAid® allows you to tailor a home to the things you love most, like cooking with your family or entertaining friends. Full suites of appliances include many individually unique product choices, like undercounter wine cellars and single-drawer dishwashers, that brilliantly perform the specialty tasks you desire.

Jenn-Air® Brand

Jenn-Air® has long been a leader in ventilation and cooking technologies that meet high gourmet standards. And, with suites like Euro-Style Stainless, Floating Glass, Pro-Style® Stainless and Oiled Bronze, there's a Jenn-Air style for any décor.

Whirlpool® Brand

Whirlpool and Whirlpool Gold brands bring increased efficiency and productivity to your kitchen and laundry space. Features like Fast Fill Technology, PowerScour™ cleaning, Speedcook Technology and Direct Inject Wash Systems help save time and effort.

Maytag® Brand

Maytag brand appliances are sought after for their famous dependability. But with features like the Ice2O™ ice dispensing system, products like the Epic laundry pair and attractive, high-end finishes Maytag®, will distinguish any home with style and performance.

Overlay kits are available for the front of certain appliances to match the cabinetry and create a more natural look. In this kitchen the refrigerator and the warming drawer (second drawer down, left of the cooktop) almost disappear.

KitchenAid Architect® Series II

The Architect® Series II is an evolution of performance and intuitive design. By combining the best of the original Architect® Series with a host of enhancements, there's more to entice people who love to cook and entertain. The refined appearance is reflected in the robust contoured knobs, rounded corners and seamless stainless steel edges. Improved performance comes in the form of adjustable settings, intuitive displays and control graphics.

KitchenAid® Outdoor Entertaining

Whether you're looking for a grill or an entire outdoor kitchen, KitchenAid® will keep your guests coming back for more. Both built-in and freestanding grills perform wonderfully to help you cook food accurately and evenly. Options like an outdoor refreshment center, refrigerator and ice maker help you keep essential ingredients conveniently close and add even more flexibility to your space.

Maytag® Home Appliances

For generations, families have depended on Maytag® products in the laundry room. Today, you can count on us for a full range of quality laundry and kitchen appliances with features designed to help you handle the demands of busy life. Maytag's commitment to innovation is unsurpassed with industry firsts such as the Gemini® oven, the first double oven range, Ice20™ the first ice-through-the-door French Door refrigerator; and the first third rack dishwasher.

Jenn-Air® Kitchen Suites

Traditional or avant-garde. Elegant or urban. Romantic or maverick. Whatever your style, there's no better place to express it than in your home—and especially your kitchen.

Jenn-Air® appliances bring your style to life every day. Details are designed for both beauty and functionality. The curve of the handle on a wall oven, the placement of the vent on a downdraft cooktop, the smooth glide of the freezer drawer on a French door refrigerator—all are crafted to work with you at the height of your creativity.

Whirlpool® Home Appliances

For busy, active people who appreciate help in accomplishing their tasks and managing their homes, Whirlpool and Whirlpool Gold brands are sure to fit your demanding lifestyle. Whether part of a solution for the kitchen, laundry or beyond, Whirlpool® products unite style and performance. With innovative solutions to facilitate everyday chores, they help save time, manage space and achieve results with less effort.

Your Plan Set Includes...

· Exterior Elevations

Front, rear, left and right sides of the house. Shows materials, details and measurements at ¼" scale.

· Detailed Floor Plans

Show the layout of the house. Rooms and interior spaces are carefully dimensioned, windows and door sizes are noted. These plans show the location of kitchen appliances and bathroom fixtures.

· Electrical Layout

Usually included on the floor plan, shows suggested locations for electrical fixtures and outlets.

· Interior and Cabinet Elevations

These drawings show specific details and dimensions of cabinets in the kitchen, laundry room, and bathrooms. Also provides views of the fireplaces, bookcases, and built-in units.

· Foundation Plan

This plan gives the foundation layout, including support walls, excavated and unexcavated areas, if any, dimensions, notes and details. Crawlspace is our standard foundation but basement and slabs are available.

· Typical Wall Section

Shows how the walls may be constructed from footer to rafter. These sections specify the home's construction, insulation, flooring and roofing details.

· Building Sections

Important changes in floor, ceiling and roof heights or the relationship of one level to another are called out and illustrated.

· Roof Plan

Shows the overall layout and necessary details for roof construction with structural sizes. If trusses are used, it is suggested that you work with your local truss manufacturer to design your trusses to comply with local codes.

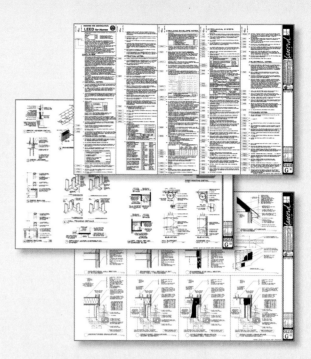

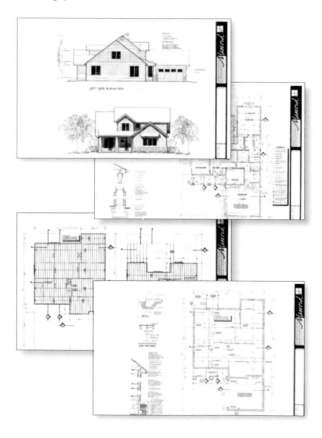

· Green (G) Sheets

These pages describe, in detail, how to construct your home to meet green building standards. Choose from two national certification tracks: LEED® or NGBS™ or a generic specification for local or uncertified projects.

· *Mascord Efficient Living* Information Supplement Packet

Information you need to build your home to be sustainable and healthy. This includes details about certification tracks, homeowners information packet, forms to give vendors, calculations, and the required forms necessary to certify your home.

· Consultation

Includes one hour phone conference or personal meeting with a Mascord Green Team member to get you on track and to answer any questions.

Efficient Living Price Guide

	B	C	D	E	F	G	H
5-Set Package	$800	845	875	925	1,000	1,075	1,175
8-Set Package	$845	900	950	1,025	1,100	1,200	1,300
Repeat 5-Set Package	$525	575	625	675	750	825	925
Repeat 8-Set Package	$575	625	675	725	800	875	975
Basement Foundation	$195	225	250	275	295	325	350
Slab Foundation	$80	95	105	125	140	160	185

Full Reverse Sets | $75 per order
Text Reads Correctly

Shipping & Handling | $15—Ground $30—2nd Day Air $50—Overnight

If you have any questions, please contact our knowledgeable sales staff.

Please note: The prices above include the Green Package.

The Plans

As a minimum, our homes are designed for 25 psf snow load, 2 x 6 exterior walls with R-21 insulation, and ceiling insulation shown as R-38 at flat areas and R-30 at vaulted areas. Regional construction practices may necessitate alteration of the drawings. Consult a local designer or engineer. A set of reproducibles or CAD files are available to facilitate this process.

The plans in the Mascord Collection are protected under the Federal Copyright Act, Title 17 of the United States Code. The purchaser agrees that the use of the plan is for one time only and that the plan or any part of it will not be reproduced by any means without the written consent of the copyright owner. Multi-use licenses are available.

Although we make every effort to ensure the accuracy of our plan information, we reserve the right to make any necessary changes to correct mistakes or make the plan comply with new building codes. Sometimes these changes will result in minor square footage discrepancies.

All prices and specifications are subject to changes without notice. Not responsible for typographic errors. Check your local building codes for design compliance and suitability on your particular site. All sales are final.

Acknowledgements

We personally wish to thank you for taking the time to learn more about *Mascord Efficient Living*, and considering building a more sustainable lifestyle. The fact that you are reading this book proves that you are one of the leaders in your community. We all understand that building a sustainable home is a large project. It takes hours of preparation and a major commitment from all the members of your team to reach your desired goal. The creation of this book is no exception. Designed to ease the process of building your efficient home, the Mascord Efficient Living program is the result of the dedication and support from all the members of our team at Alan Mascord Design Associates, our families and friends. A special thanks goes to Bob Greenspan and the other photographers whose work brings this book to life.

We wish to thank Mark Johnson, Joseph Sharkey, Daniel Page-Wood and the team at Whirlpool Corporation, whose unyielding support, vision, and commitment helped us realize our goal. Thanks to all the vendors, builders and homeowners that provided content for us to use throughout the book. We would also like to thank Randy Hansell and all the team members at Earth Advantage, Inc., for providing us with information and support throughout our journey. The work Randy has put into the development of the LEED® for Homes program, as well as his wealth of experience with Earth Advantage programs, was a huge benefit to us all.

Thanks to all those involved with qualifying the theory contained in these pages; especially our builders and development partners. Special thanks to Lockie Homes and Blazer Development, Inc., for beautifully and masterfully turning our designs into reality with their own touch of craftsmanship. Thanks to Tracy Schmitt of Lakeside Custom Homes for working with our prototype and educating us along the way. Thanks to Seabrook Development for working with us and letting us participate in the realization of their own vision, and thanks to Eric Schnell and Judge Kemp, whose homes continue to inspire. We would like to thank every homeowner living in an efficient home for protecting the future for all our children, and finally Sarah Susanka, whose work and words are an inspiration to all.

—*The Mascord Green Team*